HOW TO
OUT-SELL
OUT-MARKET
OUT-PROMOTE
OUT-ADVERTISE
EVERYONE ELSE YOU
COMPETE AGAINST...
BEFORE THEY EVEN KNOW
WHAT HIT THEM

**Powerful Strategies, Methods, Concepts, and Techniques to
Rapidly Increase Your Sales, Multiply Your Profits, and
Skyrocket Your Personal Wealth**

PAUL GORMAN

Big Sur Publishing
London, England

THIRD EDITION

Published by Big Sur Publishing
London, England

ISBN 0 9532666 2 5

Printed in Great Britain by
Redwood Books, Trowbridge, Wiltshire

4 2 1 1 6

Catalogue Data

Gorman, Paul F.
     How to Out-Sell, Out-Market, Out-Promote,
     Out-Advertise Everyone Else You Compete
     Against Before They Even Know What
     Hit Them

     1. Business Success 2. Marketing 3. Advertising

*Big Sur Publishing provides books at special discounts to use as
premiums, sales promotions, or for use in training programmes.
For further information write to:*
Sales Manager, Big Sur Publishing
212 Piccadilly, London W1V 9LD.

PRIVATE MARKETING CONSULTANCY
You can consult with Paul Gorman privately to help master-
mind specific sales and profit-generating strategies for your
business or professional practice. To receive details, please
write to him c/o Big Sur Publishing at the address above, or
telephone freephone 0800 731 3198.

Hundreds of businesses are attracting customers, earning more, and gaining competitive advantage by applying the powerful strategies in this book!

"It's a goldmine! Full of priceless nuggets of ideas and information that you can't afford to be without. I never realised how easy it could be to double the size (and profits) of my business. Before reading your book I would have been happy with 10% a year — and this is in a climate of ferocious competition. Quite simply — it's the best book on marketing I've ever read!"

Ray Linton
Managing Director
Cavendish Property Investments Ltd

"This book is an eye-opener to success and wealth through proven strategies — if you don't feel inspired when you read it you best check yourself for a pulse! The true test is in the results — so go ahead, apply the strategies and observe the results. Ignore any previous misconceptions you may have regarding the 'laws' of marketing and attracting more sales. This book really is a matter of a <u>true</u> understanding of what motivates people/companies to buy — Paul has a remarkable understanding — the results you will achieve are testament to his abilities as a marketing 'fountain of knowledge.'"

Charles Hallet
Partner
Expense Reduction Analysts

"Excellent... sizzling... inspiring. I am familiar with the works of Napoleon Hill, Joe Karbo, Brian Tracy, Jay Abraham, Michael Gerber etc, but Paul Gorman is the best for Britain in the world marketing growth strategies he portrays in every line of his book."

Mostyn Davis

"If I could write down everything I have learned running businesses for more than 25 years it would still only half fill the pages of Paul Gorman's book. There is no doubt that by implementing just a few of his strategies and techniques we have seen our sales increase — sales of one specific advert increased from £2,000 to £11,000 — I CALL THAT SPECTACULAR! We have bought more than 20 copies of this book to train our staff and to give to friends and business colleagues so they can benefit from it. BUY IT!"

Theo K L Van Dort
Chairman
TAS Software Plc

"Paul not only gives methods, concepts and strategies — for me more importantly he gives examples. He shares his experience. For the first time in business I am experiencing <u>real</u> growth."

Stuart Gascoyne
Mortgage Revision

DEDICATED TO JOANIE,
MY WONDERFUL WIFE

What this book can do for you:

Paul Gorman has spent nearly twenty-one years discovering what makes a business grow—and what holds it back. In this no-nonsense, application-specific book, he puts the full force of his knowledge into helping you adopt the most powerful business-building strategies and success principles ever discovered.

Here's just some of what you'll learn:

- How to take total control of your business—and results!
- Why investing in your business will make you 100-times more money than any passive investment you can name.
- How to increase your sales by up to 500%—maybe more—virtually overnight.
- How to create headlines and opening gambits that bring your riches.
- You have only 4 seconds to grab a customer's attention—here's the key.
- 16 response *words* that increase the power of your headline.
- 21 money-earning headlines—adapt them for your business!
- The greatest success principle of all time—it's virtually impossible to ever fail in business when you apply this to everything you do.
- A powerful 7-step formula that keeps customers riveted to your sales message.
- How to spot endorsements and testimonials that persuade customers to buy — and reject those that do not.
- Why it's true "the more you tell, the more you sell." The most important lesson you can ever learn about communicating to your customers or clients.
- 'Reasons-why' advertising—it will significantly increase the validity and selling strength of your letters, advertisements and brochures.
- Why every business should have a profit-generating database installed.
- 33-point check list for your business.
- The 7 biggest sales letter mistakes and how to avoid them.
- Become a customer of yours for a day—you'll be amazed what you discover!
- Why you MUST specialize to achieve outstanding growth.
- Six effective ways to ask for the order and get it!
- Five golden rules of customer targeting—use these to as much as DOUBLE your sales.
- My Secret Weapon. Not one in twenty businesses understand this critical customer philosophy. As soon as you apply it to *your* business, your sales and profits will soar through the roof.
- 10 rules for writing sales letters that make big money.
- Add *one* component to your sales letters and response will increase by up to 300%.
- 10 winning techniques to make *small* ads pay.
- 10 winning techniques to make *large* ads pay.
- How to increase response to your flyers and inserts by up to 800% !
- Revealed: How to multiply sales from brochures and catalogues.
- How to skyrocket your sales by adopting this simple method of communicating with customers.
- Analysis of a £2.4 million sales letter.
- How to double your sales—or more—by accessing other company's customers.
- How to attract 100's—1000's of new customers or clients within just weeks.
- *Plus much more!*

Let this book guide you to outstanding levels of business success and wealth. Read it again and again, do exactly as it says, and you will open the door to fabulous achievement and riches, plus a nobler, finer and satisfying life.

CONTENTS

PART • ONE

HOW TO PRIME YOUR BUSINESS FOR
MAJOR LEAGUE RESULTS

PART • TWO

HOW TO WIN NEW CUSTOMERS
BEFORE YOUR COMPETITORS

Chapter 4: Image Or Direct-Response? **41**

Chapter 5: The Million Pound Sales Key **44**

Chapter 6: How To Keep Customers Riveted To Your
Sales Message **61**

CONTENTS

CONTENTS

CONTENTS

PART • FOUR

7 Rapid Business Multipliers— How To Generate £10,000 - £100,000 New Business And Cash, Virtually Overnight

Chapter 18: Rapid Business Multiplier #1: Test And Market The Clear Winner 174

Contents

Contents

IMPORTANT NOTE

How To Use This Book
To Grow Your Business

This book is divided into four parts. Although I know you will be tempted to flick through it, and go straight to sections which apply to you most, you should, when you've finished flicking, read the whole book in order.

Why? Because this information is most powerful **only when you use it in combination.**

For instance, if you skipped right to Chapter 15: **How To Out-Advertise Every One Of Your Competitors,** without understanding the secrets of human-response found in Part 2, you'd miss out on the power of *persuasion* that enables you to write powerful ads.

The book gives you — **Part One:** a revealing understanding of your business's real potential to attract customers and generate wealth. **Part Two:** an understanding of human nature — the strategies and communication approaches that compel customers to *respond* to your sales message. **Part Three:** high-profit marketing techniques, methods and concepts you can use to rapidly build your business. **Part Four:** Cash generation — how to generate up to £10,000-£1,000,000 new business and cash, virtually overnight.

Commit to **applying** the strategies in this book. They work! Here's what I suggest: underline every passage that is important to you *as you read it* (underlining will NOT affect your 12-month money back guarantee). Tests have proven that when you underline a passage, you absorb information two-three times more effectively.

Second, take immediate **action** on each worthwhile strategy. That said, let's move on...

Introduction

Growing your business is a SCIENTIFIC process. Contrary to most professional advice, the process of attracting buying customers to your door is uncomplicated, logical, and systematic.

Fundamentally, you only need grasp one simple — *but critical* — principle, in order to build your business to almost any size and financial level you want. Nothing can stop your progress once you incorporate this foundational principle into every contact you have with customers and prospective customers.

It is this:

No matter what business you are in, you are really selling to *the same customer* as every other business: a PERSON!

Think about it. Whether you are looking to buy a bar of soap, a washing machine, a car, a copper pipeline, a PC, a holiday, a.... book!, you want the same basic fulfilment from your purchase — benefits, results, and value for money.

That's all you care about as a customer. That's all **your customers** care about when they buy from you. "Will this *really* work for me?" is the same question every customer asks every seller, no matter what they are buying. When you understand how to **market your product or service with human-response strategies** by interestingly, informatively, and educationally demonstrating the benefits, advantages, results, and value your customer can expect when buying from you, you possess the ammunition to rapidly increase your sales and multiply your bottom line profits, *by many hundreds of percent.*

Perhaps the most surprising — and exhilarating — suggestion I want to put to you is this: **You always have been, and you always will be, in total control of your business results.**

When I suggested this at one of my business-building seminars recently, an experienced businessman stood right up and said, "That's not true! Every external factor that I have no control over affects my business results, like whether the economy is booming or depressed, whether customers respond to my advertising, the cost of my overhead, what my competitors are charging!"

Of course he was correct, right?

Wrong.

I will show you how to profit in both boom and depression, how to guarantee customers respond to your advertisements, how to make so much residual money that overhead is not even a consideration, and how to gain powerful competitive advantage, almost overnight.

When you apply marketing principles, methods, techniques, and strategies that have for years proven to be more sales and profit-effective than any others, *and you recognise that your customer is king,* your business success becomes **predictable.**

My goal in writing this book is to furnish you with the precise sales-building and profit-generating strategies that will change your business from run-of-the-mill to runaway success, from marginally profitable to cash rich, from industry henchman to industry leader.

One more thing. It's important.

Many, if not all, the concepts, methods, and strategies you'll learn in this book go against 'traditional' business wisdom and teaching. You won't learn these techniques at business college, or in most marketing books, or from your peers, bank manager, or accountant.

Neither, regrettably, will you get the results I promise you if you commission an advertising agency, bar a handful.

So I ask you to keep your mind open. Don't be wedded to tradition. Your first instinct, when you see a result quoted, or a strategy that promises large, geometric increases in sales, might be to disbelieve that you can achieve the same results in your business. Don't make that mistake. Change your paradigm. Adopt a different mind-set. Become a believer of **possibility, not impossibility.**

There is no theory here. Every figure I cite, every improvement in sales and profits, are **actual results obtained by real businesses today.**

Let's now get straight on with building *your* business!

PART 1

How to Prime Your Business For Super-Success

CHAPTER 1

How To Change The Odds of Winning and Super-Charge Your Business with New Sales

Imagine you could change the rules of doing business. Imagine you could influence every sales process, marketing strategy, promotional event, and advertising campaign you ever undertake, *in your favour,* so the odds of you winning... and generating substantially higher sales and bottom line profits... were multiplied up to *many hundreds of times.*

Equally, imagine if you could reduce, or eliminate entirely, the risk you take as a business owner. What if there were a set of sales-multiplying strategies sufficiently powerful and profit-driven to make your success ***predictable?***

Impossible, right?

WRONG!

You CAN change the rules of business so the odds of winning are in your favour. More than that, you can apply marketing strategies, concepts, methods and principles that will change the performance of your business, virtually overnight.

When you apply the marketing procedures that, for years, have proven to be more sales and profit-efficient than any others identified, your success indeed will be predictable.

Too bold a statement? Consider this.

Eighteen months ago, the proprietor of a computer company asked me to help him grow his business. He designs and builds PC's and provides maintenance contracts for office machinery. He'd been in business seventeen years and built an impressive list of high profile clients, including a number of well known national companies.

But although he'd attempted various ways to gain new customers his response was disappointing. What could he do?

After seeing his marketing I realised the problem. He was marketing himself *in the same way 95 percent of his competitors were marketing themselves.*

What distinguishes one business from another when nearly every company in an industry markets themselves in fundamentally the same way? This company was saying: we offer a good product and service, buy from *us!* They received little response from this approach. Hundreds of computer companies claim they sell quality PC's, at competitive prices, with good service. He was only one in a big crowd of businesses trying to wave down passing customers.

I suggested he use a strategy that would give him immediate competitive advantage, and position his company favourably in the eyes of his prospective customers.

For less than £1,000 spent on marketing the strategy his turnover increased by 31 percent in just six weeks.

It was not difficult to implement. It was not costly. It was just a strategy that made his success predictable. **You can use it in your business too.** (See Chapter 13.)

Another entrepreneur who ran a secretarial training school wanted to know how to increase response from her advertising. Her ads were pulling only four or five new students a week, not enough to pay for themselves, nor to grow her business.

But, like most businesses I see, her ads were *institutional* not *direct response.* They didn't grab her prospect's attention, provide a compelling reason to respond, or ask for action. They simply stated her school's name, listed courses available, and gave an address and telephone number. But this wasn't enough to compel students to take her courses! Consequently, her advertising was largely a waste of resources.

When the ad was rewritten, her response skyrocketed by **400 percent** within seven days. Bear in mind, the ad was the same size; it cost her not a penny more but her response was now four times higher. Instead of five students from each ad she now got twenty. This was possible because she used a marketing strategy that made her success predictable. **You can increase response to your advertisements, too.** (See Chapter 15.)

A young client of mine owns a hair styling and beauty therapy salon. It is well positioned on the high street, she is highly qualified, and her existing clients are loyal to the salon.

But try as she would, only a trickle of new clients came into the salon each month. To make matters tougher, there were five competing salons in her street, each of which seemed to have more money to market with than she did.

She wasn't getting anywhere.

Like most businesses with competitors on the doorstep, she needed to gain competitive advantage. What she didn't understand at the time was how straightforward it usually is.

Until this time, she had tried advertising to bring in new clients, as her five competitors did. Only their ads were bigger and more impressive.

So I suggested a simple strategy that no other salon was using. The result? She gained powerful competitive advantage almost overnight, and increased her turnover 22 percent in four weeks. Now, whenever she wants additional clients she simply repeats the strategy. Her competitors are scratching their heads wondering how she is attracting all the business while they continue to run big, fancy — *and costly* — advertisements with marginal response.

She won a stream of new clients because she applied a marketing strategy that made her success predictable. **You can do the same in your business.** (See Chapter 13: letter #3, plus Chapter 23: Rapid Business Multiplier #6.)

You do not have to 'gamble' to win customers — **if you use proven, time-tested, profit-driven, sales-multiplying strategies.** You never have to only 'hope' to significantly boost your sales and increase your profits. You don't ever have to just 'wish' you could succeed.

Gambling, hoping and wishing doesn't play any part in it. You can take quantum leaps forward if, *and as soon as,* you apply principles that cannot fail to grow your business.

How To Apply These Business-Building Strategies To *Your* Business

These principles work in any business. And I do mean **any.**

Do you believe that? Surely, selling insurance is different to selling clothes? Selling houses is different to selling computers. Selling memberships to a health club is different to selling tables at a restaurant? If you believe that, you are right... and wrong!

Selling houses *is* different to selling computers. **But the principle of persuading prospects to respond to your sales message is the same.**

When you understand how to compel prospects with your sales message, and you apply those principles to the idiosyncrasies of your particular business, you win more buying customers.

Why? Because the principles of human-response are **scientific.** Just as the law of gravity applies all over the planet, whether you are a good or bad person, whether the economy is sluggish or bullish, whether you are in Britain, the USA, Australia, or Fiji, so the law of human-response applies to all customers. We'd all be in chaos if gravity suddenly decided to stop working because a very important person was about to fall from a tall building. Gravity won't stop working for anybody. So you'd better watch out for it!

So it is with human-response. When you use the principles and specific strategies that I'll show you, you increase the odds in your favour. Attracting customers becomes a *certainty*.

I Challenge You To Grow Your Business NOW!

I challenge you to apply the business-building strategies, concepts, principles and methods revealed in this book, and see your venture grow exponentially. Have no doubt: You can take major, **major** leaps forward when you apply the specifics I'll show you.

Every year approximately 450,000 people in the UK start a business. 56 percent fail within the first three years. Two years later the failures rise to **76 percent.** Sadly most of these businesses had a good idea, a good product, or a good service. You can have a great product, and fail. You can have a second-rate product, and succeed.

It's not only your idea, product, or service that counts. *It's how you market yourself* that creates the titanic difference between runaway success, and mediocrity, or failure.

Most businesses never succeed in growing to the size they quite easily could, or they fail, **because they use strategies that make it *difficult* for them to succeed.**

They never reach their potential because they don't understand the strategies that would virtually guarantee their success. They assume it's difficult and expensive to acquire new customers in a competitive market. But it's simple when you adopt and apply proven sales-winning techniques.

Over the years, I have spoken to *hundreds* of business owners. Here are the top five challenges they quote as being difficult to tackle:

- Business is slow. Customers are cautious about spending money.
- I don't know *how* to acquire more customers.
- Competitors are selling on price—I can't compete at rock-bottom prices without going bust.
- I haven't got the financial resources I need to market my business effectively.
- I am in a catch-22. I need extra staff to grow but I cannot afford the salaries.

All valid reasons. But when you look at their marketing you realise these businesses are *keeping customers away* with punitive sales attempts. They erect a barrier between themselves and prospective buyers. Unknowingly, they make it *difficult* not *easy* for customers to buy from them.

A self-made multimillionaire who grew a fledgling carpet shop into California's largest carpet and flooring supplier with thirty-six outlets told me, "If all this was taken away from me tomorrow, and I was left with no money at all, I could start over and within twelve months, I'd be a millionaire again."

He understood human nature. He knew how to compel customers with his sales messages. He realised the importance of giving **value.** He could repeat the 'formula' without any start-up capital and customers would once again flock to his door.

These pages reveal how to engineer your own business supremacy, create mammoth sales and profit leverage, and provide you personally with rich financial rewards. You'll discover how to win more customers than you've dreamed of, realise how to garner additional sales from your existing customers, how to increase the average worth of each sale, how to create multiple profit-centres, arrange high-profit joint ventures and host/recipient alliances, engineer large cash windfalls from hidden assets within your business, become a customer-oriented organisation. You'll discover how **adding value** to every sale attracts ten times the number of customers.

And you'll see how to position yourself as a leader within your market and ride profitably through even the most competitive and economically challenging conditions.

The challenge is set! I know what amount of financial value the information on these pages is worth to your business — and to you personally. Apply the secrets I'll share with you and you will reap high rewards.

Read how each strategy will produce higher sales and improved profits. Then start *applying the strategies to your particular business situation.* As you introduce them, and keep on applying them, your business will grow exponentially, gain leadership, stability and poise within your market, accumulate large cash resources, and provide you with the competitive advantage you are looking for.

Turn the page now to discover: **The Key To Super-Growth Most Business Owners Overlook...**

CHAPTER 2

The Key To Super-Growth
Most Business Owners Overlook

If I asked you, "What is your business?" you might reply the *computer* business, or the *restaurant* business, or the *steel tube* business, or the *airline* business, or the *photographic processing* business, or the *vitamin supplements* business, or the *fashion* business, or whatever business yours is.

But if you answered by telling me what business you are 'in', I would know you are probably **holding your business back** from growing as successfully as it could.

The good news is you can correct this subtle — *but critical* — mistake very quickly. I have seen miracle changes and new sales occur within weeks as soon as a business owner realises the simple but largely overlooked key to super-growing any business.

What is it?

**Whatever your type of trade, service, or profession,
never... ever... work 'in' it.**

What do you do if you don't work *in* it?

You work 'on' it.

A businessman telephoned me once in desperation. He was in the kitchen refitting business.

He told me he manufactured high quality kitchen units and because he sold them direct to the public, cutting out the middle man, he was able to sell at lower prices than most of his competitors. Yet his sales were slow and he was rapidly losing money.

He was frustrated and dismayed. *What was he doing wrong?*

After listening to him explain his business, I told him he was working 'in' it, not 'on' it.

He had a good product. He was selling at competitive prices. But he was viewing his business from an *internal perspective* not an *external perspective.*

He was too involved in the minute-to-minute, everyday running of his enterprise, instead of allocating some specific time each week to marketing his business.

To paraphrase Joe Karbo, the late marketing genius and self made millionaire, *he was too busy earning a living to make any money.*

Most entrepreneurs, directors, and professionals I see are too busy running their business to make any money.

How To Change From Working 'In' Your Business To Working 'On' It

To understand how to change from working 'in' your business to working 'on' it, and to multiply your results, throw open your imagination. Use your mind to play a game.

Imagine you are playing the board game, Monopoly™. Imagine you could shrink your body to the size of one of the game pieces on the board.

You'd notice tall buildings; huge, oversized piles of money; you'd be moved from one end of the board to the other without your consent. You'd be wheeled and dealt by someone controlling *you.*

You'd be **'in'** the game.

Now imagine you enlarge yourself to full size again and take control of the game. Now **you** control the moves. **You** make the deals. **You** evaluate the board situation and make your moves based on what you think will profit you most.

You are now working **'on'** the game. You're no longer a game piece, you're a **game player—in control.**

Do you see the difference? Do you think you'd win more games controlling the board from above, rather than being one of the game pieces? Of course! You are *significantly* more effective playing from above.

The same is true of your business.

Millions of pounds are made by savvy entrepreneurs buying an ailing business at a knock-down price, increasing its value with effective marketing, and selling it at large profit.

Why is one entrepreneur able to succeed while the founder failed? *Because the founder was too attached to his or her venture.*

If you hold dear your product or service, or you don't recognise the absolute need to systematically market what you're selling, you can mistakenly assume *customers* will recognise it's value without being presented with the full sales story. That very rarely happens!

To succeed you have to market your products or services with interesting, compelling, believable sales messages that evoke a buying response.

Understand This Key And You're On Your Way To Big Success

In order to grow your business successfully, always—everyday, every hour—work **on** it, not in it.

What do you work on? Work on **marketing** your product or service.

You're not in the business of computers, or restaurants, or steel tubes, or vitamin supplements, or whatever—you are really in the business of *marketing*.

This is the key to geometrically growing a business that most owners, directors and professionals overlook. Whenever you see a business out-selling its competitors, don't scratch your head thinking, "If only I had their product or service, I'd be selling high volumes too." No, look at their *marketing!*

> *Marketing your business is the powerful key to creating*
> *all the success and wealth you could ever want.*
> *When you market your business you are working on it,*
> *and you'll reap one hundred times more reward*
> *than if you keep working in it.*

One caveat: The marketing keys I am showing you are highly

effective sales and profit multipliers. The strategies, concepts and principles you'll learn are responsible for millions of pounds of additional sales throughout a diverse range of companies and industries.

Unfortunately, they work as effectively on *bad* products or services as they do on *good* ones, at least initially. So, in knowing how to generate high response you have a responsibility to yourself and your customers.

I am sure you are honest and are interested in giving good value. Of course, you'll be far more successful, and far wealthier, selling good value than you ever will selling bad quality or valueless products.

But if you were dishonest you would... initially... be able to sell high volumes with good marketing. Why? Because **marketing is the key.**

Why Bad Businesses Often Succeed And Great Businesses Often Fail

You've seen bad products sell consistently. You've seen great products bomb. It is all down to how they are *marketed.*

You can use effective marketing to sell high volumes of good... and, unfortunately, bad... products.

And you can use ineffective marketing on a great product, and it will be doomed to mediocrity or failure.

You might have heard about the coat-hook scandal some years ago. An unscrupulous businessman placed an advert in a national advertiser selling a new design of coat hook. **"Hang your coats anywhere in the house — on any door or wall — with these attractive new, easy to fix hooks. 10 hooks just £3,"** promised the advert.

A few *thousand* people bought the hooks, for the publication had over one million readers. But when customers received their package, all they got was ten steel door nails.

Not surprisingly, the trickster had to flee when he was bombarded by angry customers.

Does effective marketing work, even on a bad product? Absolutely! Is it worth trying to make a quick buck dishonestly?

Absolutely not. Had this rogue offered genuine, good value coat hooks he could have continued advertising and made a lot more money. His ad worked well!

The key to optimum business success is to offer the best value product or service you can afford, market it powerfully, ensure your customers are satisfied, and sell your back-end repeatedly.

Always remember, what determines how successful you will be is not so much to do with your product or service, **it's how well you market it.**

What difference will marketing really make to your sales, bottom line profits, and to your personal wealth? Turn to the next chapter to find out...

CHAPTER 3

Marketing Your Business
Is The Greatest Investment
You Can Ever Make

There is not a faster or more effective system of creating wealth for yourself than through the powerful process of **marketing your business.**

When it boils down to fundamentals, you are in business to make money. Hopefully you have a product or service that you enjoy selling, even cherish.

But when it comes time to go home at the end of the week, and you've been honest and ethical in your dealings with customers, you want to be in a position to take the largest financial payoff for your effort that you personally desire, or need.

More than this, I believe it is your *responsibility* as a business owner to create wealth for the livelihood of yourself, your family, your employees, your vendors, your suppliers, and your community.

These people rely on you either totally or in part for their livelihoods. By creating wealth—by optimizing your business performance and generating the highest possible profit returns for your efforts—you not only increase the quality and capability of *your* life and the life of your family, you play a significant role in increasing the quality and capabilities of your employees and vendors lives, and those in your community.

I believe in **optimum performance.** Why have an asset lying in your business that isn't producing the highest profit-return it is capable of? Or isn't producing any profit at all?

Right now your business has hidden assets you can gain

powerful leverage on within days or weeks. The biggest of those are your customers themselves.

But most businesses I see market themselves so *ineffectively*, they drive customers away in droves, rather than attract them in masses.

Imagine! Did you ever think your sales approach could be *driving prospective customers away*, allowing them to give money to your competitors? I see marketing every day that is doing just that.

When you use interesting, informative, compelling, educational, ethical marketing, and you apply it to every asset in your business, then customers will beat a path to your door, and you will generate more wealth, more efficiently, more quickly.

If You Want To Make a Million Pounds There Are Two Ways You Can Succeed

If you want to become financially independent, there are basically two ways you can achieve it: you can invest in a passive growth vehicle—stocks or shares or property, for instance.

Or you can generate it yourself by marketing your business.

I want to suggest that you can create far more wealth, more rapidly, in a business of your own, than you ever can by investing in stocks, shares, or property.

If you invest in stocks or shares, just as you can make a profitable return on your investment, you can also, of course, lose your investment. *There's a direct correlation between risk and return.*

But when you invest in marketing your business, you may be surprised to learn **you have very little risk, or no risk at all.**

Why? Because stocks and shares are a passive investment; you have no control over the growth of your money. If you invest £100,000, along with the potential to *make* money, you risk making *no* money if the market remains stagnant, or losing your entire £100,000 if the stocks you've invested in fail.

You Don't Have To Wait For Success!

Do you want more money to improve the quality of your life **now?** Then don't invest in stocks or shares! Generally, if you want a fairly low-risk stock investment (I would!) it takes **years** for you to gain on your capital.

Are you impatient for results? Are you a *now* person? I know I am. I want results *now!* I don't want to wait forever for things to happen. Particularly where business and financial success are concerned.

If there's a faster way of multiplying sales, an overlooked method of winning new customers, a more efficient system of amassing cash resources, I want to know about it and apply it **right away!**

How You Can Invest And Make £1,000,000+

If you are willing to invest long-term, you can put money in reasonably safe trusts—Unit Trusts—and reap considerably higher returns than is possible from any high street.

Unit Trusts (Mutual Funds in the US) have proven to be amongst the highest returning 'safe' investments. Over the last twenty-five years, top performing funds have produced an average return for their investors of between 16 - 21 percent.

But even if you invested £200 a month—£6.60 a day—with a 20 percent annual compound growth on capital, it would take you ten years to get £75,219, fifteen years to get £233,140, twenty years to get £621,930, and twenty-five years to get £1,697,057.

Don't get me wrong, £1,700,000 is a lot of money. But twenty-five years is a long time to wait for it if there is a faster way.

Your Business Has The Leverage To Out-Perform Any Investment!

But in business **you are in control of your results.** You can accumulate wealth considerably faster.

You always have been, and **you always will be,** in total control of your business results.

If you invest £100,000 in your business, and you use specific, profit-driven marketing strategies to grow your enterprise, you can reap a return of £150,000, £200,000, £300,000, £500,000, £1,000,000 or more, substantially faster.

How? Your business always has, and always will have, the ability to generate up to *hundreds of percent* return on your investment, with very low risk, or no risk at all.

Here's an example.

Let's say you are in the pet food business — you make premium dog food and sell it in tins to retailers nationally.

You run an advert in a prominent retail trade magazine to encourage more stores to stock your tins.

Your advert costs £1,000. Each box, consisting of six tins of food, costs the retailer £5 to buy, from which you make £2 profit. Currently, you sell an average of 575 boxes from every advert. So you make £150 profit. (575 boxes x £2 profit = £1,150 minus £1,000 ad cost = £150 profit.)

Now what if I could show you how to increase the number of boxes you sell without increasing the size of your ad?

What if I showed you seven key elements your advert was missing that would significantly increase your response?

With the right elements of response in your advert, your sales can increase by 50 percent, 100 percent, 200 percent, 500 percent, or more. Results of this magnitude are everyday events when direct response strategies are applied to institutional advertising.

Massive increases in response are being achieved by businesses applying these strategies. Amongst the most powerful response-multipliers you can use in your marketing are **headlines.**

You'll see how straightforward it is to add £1,000's, £10,000's, £100,000's, or £1,000,000's to your sales with powerful, benefit-oriented headlines. (See Chapter 5.)

But in case you accuse me of being over-enthusiastic let's be conservative. What happens when you apply a few of the marketing techniques you'll learn in the following chapters to your dog food advert.

Let's say by including a compelling headline, an interesting and persuasive sales story, a risk-reversal guarantee, and a call-to-action, your sales from each advert increase by 50 percent. Here's what would happen:

Previously you were making £150 profit per £1,000 advert. In other words, you were achieving a 15 percent growth on your money: (£1,000 to £1,150 = 15%.) Not bad.

Your new advert increases your sales by 50 percent. Now you sell 863 boxes instead of 575. Your profit is boosted from £150 to **£726** per advert — a **484% increase in profit** on the same £1,000 investment (863 boxes x £2 profit = £1,726 minus £1,000 ad cost = £726 profit.)

You have increased your return on investment simply by recognising and gaining leverage on an asset you already have — in this case, your advertising.

Always remember: **You always have been, and you always will be, in total control of your business results.**

You can — at any time — switch your business *on* or *off* to suit your circumstances. You are in control.

What if you tested various other adverts, and your response increased by 100 percent, or two hundred percent, or more? Your profit would skyrocket even further.

Where else can you influence the outcome of your investment by applying growth strategies that increase the return you receive?

No other investment I know of provides you with the same leverage. No passive investment can earn equally high returns within just weeks or months, with little or no risk.

What other opportunity in life gives you the ability to compound your profits month after month, year after year, by such large multiples?

In the early Eighties I was selling an audio home study course on how to play rock and jazz-rock guitar. It was the first 'interactive' home study course available.

When students completed each lesson, they were asked to record a musical assignment on cassette tape and return it for a recorded critique and helpful hints on how to improve their playing. A live guitarist would also play examples on their tape.

I placed adverts in the national music press asking readers

to cut a coupon and send for a free information pack. The headline I used was:

Rock
Guitar
Course

The ads were making a profit. But I wondered if I could generate more response without enlarging the ad or spending more money. So I wrote and tested five different headlines that I thought would motivate budding players to send for details of the course.

Two of them produced *less* response than I was getting already. One pulled about the same. One pulled a little more. But one pulled a massive **500 percent more response.**

Overnight I was receiving five times more inquiries every time I placed the ad. Bear in mind the size and cost of my ad was the same.

From that day on I realised the tremendous leveraging power you have as a business owner when you understand that marketing is the key.

What was the winning headline? Here it is:

Be A Successful
Lead Guitarist...
Earn While You Learn

One company selling English language courses changed the headline of their advert from,

The Man Who Simplified English

to,

Do You Make These Mistakes In English?

The new headline pulled 300 percent more response than the previous one.

An Insurance company tested two different headlines for a

lower cost motor insurance for drivers with a good driving history. The headlines were:

Auto Insurance At Lower Rates
If You Are A Good Driver

and,

How To Turn Your Careful Driving Into Money

The first headline pulled an incredible 1,200 percent more than the second.

Apply These Sales-Boosting Strategies To *Every* Area Of Your Business

Never doubt you can boost your advertising results by quantum leaps when you apply simple, but powerful, marketing techniques.

But it doesn't only apply to your advertising! *Every* area of your business can generate higher profits. Whether you are advertising, sending sales letters, brochures, flyers, blow-ins, direct mail, one, two, or three-step selling, using telemarketing, employing sales people... every area of your business can be recognised as a leveragable asset, and coerced into producing a higher profit.

That is why I suggest **marketing your business gives you the greatest investment opportunity.**

YOU Are In Total Control Of Your Business Results

Most business owners, directors and professionals are not aware that **they** control their business results. In owning a business, **you control your success and your ultimate destiny.**

Most believe they are at the mercy of circumstances they have little control over. If sales are slow they presume they can't do much to change them. If no one comes into their store they think there's no other way of selling. If a new product fails to make an impact on consumers they say it's the fault of the product, not the marketing.

But external circumstances do not control your results. <u>You</u> control your results by the effectiveness of your marketing. *How* **you market your product or service is the key to how prosperous your business becomes.**

Not one in twenty businesses I see uses savvy, direct-response marketing strategies that enable them to optimize their performance. When *you* apply them, not only will you multiply your results, but your competitors won't understand how you're doing it. It won't make sense to them. They believe there isn't an alternative, more effective way.

Right now, commit every element of your business to the strategies of peak performance. Understand that marketing and optimizing your assets provides you with the ultimate investment opportunity. Realise that you are in control of that opportunity.

In my seminars I show business owners, company directors and professionals how to grow their ventures up to tenfold over twelve to twenty months, using the strategies in this book. You can do the same.

Marketing is the key to all the sales, growth, industry leadership, and cash resources you ever want... and *need...* to compete successfully in today's environment.

Now let's get specific in Part 2: **How To Win New Customers Before Your Competitors...**

PART 2

How to Win New Customers Before Your Competitors

CHAPTER 4

Image Or Direct-Response: What Do Customers Respond To First?

Most print, radio and TV ads, brochures, sales letters, flyers, blow-ins, inserts, card decks I see are largely a waste of cash resources. Businesses ceaselessly broadcast unconvincing sales messages hoping to capture new customers. Most of these — unbeknown to those who write them — are so ineffective at persuading a prospect to buy, they waste 80 or 90 percent of the cash spent on them.

Most marketing I see in the UK, USA, and Europe is 'institutional' or 'image' marketing. It portrays a selfish *me-the-business* message instead of an altruistic *you-the-customer* message.

It says to prospects: Buy what I am selling. Give *me* your money instead of a competitor." Messages like this are largely ignored. They may look graphically appealing, or they may amuse your prospects, but they don't compel them to **buy.**

From the very first time stone age man traded a club or flint with his neighbour, the only thing he was interested in was *"What's in it for me?"* There's no way he wandered up to the club-makers cave wanting to know what business name the bearded one traded under, what beautiful wood carving went into his club making, or how long his enterprise had been established. **All** he wanted to know was, *"How is this club going to help me clobber my next meal?"*

Not much has changed! In most respects human nature is the same today. All your customers want to know is, "What's in it for me?" They're screaming, "Tell me the **benefits** of your product or service, and show me the **advantage** I will gain, and I'll buy large quantities from you."

41

As a business owner trying to sell as many of your products or services as possible, the nearer you get to specifically answering the *What's in it for me?* question, the more you will sell.

Institutional or image marketing does not come close to compelling a prospect to buy from you? Why? Because it fails to persuasively demonstrate the benefits and advantages your product or service offers. It doesn't *lead your prospect through the sale* to the point of purchase.

How To Grab Prospects Attention And Lead Them To Buy Your Product

Since the early 1900s, tens of thousands of market tests, and millions of pounds of investment, have proved unarguably that **direct-response** sales messages out-pull institutional marketing by large margins. Customers and prospects respond in significantly greater numbers to a direct, specific, compelling, and detailed sales message, than to a glitzy institutional *me*-message.

Any piece of marketing, advertising or promotion that does not evoke some form of immediate response from your reader, listener, or viewer, either as an inquiry or a sale, is at worst a blatant waste of your cash resources, and at best not able to produce the considerably higher response you could receive *for no extra expenditure.*

The Folly of Institutional Marketing

Institutional marketing is what most businesses produce. Typically they will create an advert with their company or product name emblazoned across the top, a list and perhaps photographs of what they sell, prices, an 'established since...' statement, with their address and telephone number at the bottom.

They are saying *here we are, this is what we sell, this is the price, and here's where you can buy it.* But just presenting me with your product and its price isn't going to persuade me to buy it.

This type of marketing will hardly, if ever, recover its production cost let alone generate an optimum profit.

Think about it. When have you ever bought a product after

simply seeing it? Before you buy something, you want to discover as much about it as you can—what it will do for you, how it will benefit, help, enrich, make easier, faster, better, your life or your work or your play or your relationship, how long it will last, why it is better than a competing product, whether it will really do what you want it to do.

Institutional marketing doesn't answer these questions.

Change Your Institutional Marketing To *Direct-Response* and Multiply Your Sales Exponentially

When you change your marketing from institutional to **direct-response** you will see your sales increase exponentially, *for no extra cost.* You can invest £1,000, or £10,000, or £100,000, or £1,000,000 and turn it into £10,000, £100,000, £1,000,000 or £10,000,000. Direct response marketing gives you the power to invest your money, and garner a rapid profit-return of up to *hundreds of percent,* or more.

Do you fully understand this? **With the same marketing pound,** you can multiply your response from marginal or unprofitable, to highly profitable. *You don't need extra cash to reap dramatically higher sales and profits from every sales message you put out.*

What is direct-response marketing? It is giving your prospect or customer enough of your full sales story to compel him or her to take action and inquire about, or buy whatever it is you are selling.

It provides sufficient, persuasive sales information to evoke an immediate response from your reader, listener, or viewer. It stirs up interest, creates desire, fulfils needs, and leads your prospect or customer into taking action now.

Turn the page to discover what gives your sales message its most persuasive appeal: **The Million-Pound Sales Secret...**

CHAPTER 5

The Million-Pound Sales Secret

Years ago, when I was a struggling entrepreneur trying to make a success of my first business, I drove a cab to make extra money. Little did I know while ferrying people around town I was just about to learn a million pound sales secret.

One day I picked up a friendly but rough-looking guy who said to me, " 'ow much to the station, mate?" I told him the price and he said, "Blimey, that's cheap! Give me the name of your cab company so I can put it in my phone and book you everyday." I gave him the name but it was too long. His mobile would only accept nine digits. So he said, "Come on mate, what can I put you in as?" Before I could think of an alternative he said, "I know, I'll put you in as CHEAPCABS."

And there it is. **Cheap Cabs.** *All* this guy wanted to know was that the cab company was cheap. He didn't give a darn what the company name was, or how nice we were, or how long we had been established, or how new the car was. *Just that we would charge him less money than other cab companies for the same journey.*

For this customer, CHEAP CABS said it all.

As for me, I always thank this stranger for giving me a million pound sales lesson — **the power of creating compelling, benefit-oriented headlines.**

The first key to generating thousands, hundreds of thousands, or millions of pounds of sales is creating powerful **headlines** for your sales messages. You must grab your prospect's attention and compel him or her to buy your product.

An attention-getting headline at the top of your print adverts; the first words spoken in your radio or TV advert; the first sentence uttered by your salespeople or telemarketing people; the headline, first sentence or first paragraph of your sales letter, brochure, flyer, insert, or blow-in. You must capture your prospect's interest immediately, or you've lost the chance to 'sell' to him or her. You could spend hours writing the best, most descriptive, most appealing, most persuasive sales description, but unless you first capture your prospect's interest your efforts are futile.

In just a few seconds you have to captivate and interest your reader, listener, or viewer with a powerful headline statement.

You Have Only 4 Seconds to Capture Your Prospect's Interest

Four seconds is all you've got — maximum. Often, it's just one or two seconds. Here's what happens in your customer's mind when you are vying for his or her attention amongst the bevy of other sales messages they're being bombarded with:

Pick up any newspaper or magazine. Start glancing through it just as you would normally. Now stop at the **first article** that catches your eye.

Now think. How long did it take you to find that *particular* article? First, you scanned each page looking for an article you'd be interested in reading. How long did you take you to scan each page? A matter of **seconds,** right? Let's assume you found an article that interested you on Page 3. It probably took you about 3 to 10 seconds to decide you didn't want to read anything on page one, and about 3 to 10 seconds on page two. In those 3 to 10 seconds, how many articles did you skip because they didn't interest you? Six per page? Maybe ten? Let's say six. So to get to the article that **did** catch your eye on Page 3, you scanned **but ignored** at least twelve articles in less than twenty seconds — 1.6 seconds per article.

Tests have confirmed you only have 1 to 4 seconds to capture your customer's interest.

Now think further. *Why* did you stop at that particular article? What caught your eye? Was it the editorial? Was it the name of the journalist? Was it the layout of the article on the page? No! The only reason you stopped at that article was because the **headline caught your attention.**

Even if other articles *could* have interested you, you didn't stop at them because those headlines failed to grab your attention or interest.

There is no difference between what compels people to read, listen, or watch editorial or interest features, than what compels them to read, listen, or watch your sales messages.

If you fail to capture your customer's or prospect's attention instantly, you've lost them.

A powerful headline is the number one key to maximising sales. You could be selling the greatest product or service on the planet, but if no one notices your sales message you're not going to get rich.

Create compelling, attention-grabbing, benefit-oriented headlines for all your marketing, in every media you use. **Then you'll get your sales message noticed.**

One Headline Can Out-Sell Another By Hundreds of Percent

Amazingly, **90 percent** of the reason customers and prospects respond to a sales message is because of what they have read, heard, or seen in the **headline** or **opening statement.**

A moment ago you stopped at the news item only because the **headline** caught your interest. Not the editorial. Your customers will respond to your sales message for the same reason. They will only read or listen to your offer if you give them with a powerful, interesting headline.

Make an indelible mental note of this — write it on a big piece of card and fix it above your desk — remind yourself of it everyday: **90 percent of the response you get is because of your headline.**

To put it another way, if you fail to create a compelling headline you are banking up to *only one tenth* of the sales you could be.

An effective headline doesn't cost you any more money than an ineffective headline, or no headline. But an effective headline added to an already good sales appeal can generate up to hundreds of percent additional response.

How a Powerful Headline Is Created

If I arrived at your office one day and said, "Hello, I'm John Smith," you would say *so what?* and show me the way out.

If I arrived and said, "Hello, I'm John Smith, can I interest you in office stationery?" even though I've now revealed what my business is, you are still likely to show me the door. Why? *Because I haven't given you a **reason** to be interested in what I am selling.*

Yet this is how most businesses approach their marketing. They plaster their company name at the top of their ads. They simply state the name of their product or service. Hundreds, thousands, or tens of thousands of customers who could benefit from their offer and who could be motivated to buy it, ignore it instead because the sales message does not capture their interest, or show the *benefit* they would obtain.

But if I arrived at your office and said, "Hello, my name is John Smith, and I'd like to show you how I can provide all the stationery your office uses all year for typically **half the price you are buying it at now** — same brands, same-day free delivery, plus every item you buy has a no-questions, 90-day money-back guarantee if you're not 100% delighted..." and then I went on to prove that this indeed was the case, and that as an average sized business you could save in the region of £2,000 to £5,000 a year on your stationery costs, **you are more likely to be interested, aren't you?**

You would be more interested because I've now provided you with a good reason to be.

At the very least, you are significantly more *likely* to respond to my offer.

Can you see the difference? Can you see how a targeted, specific, headline or opening statement will reach out to your prospects, interest them, motivate them, and compel them to read, listen to, or watch your sales message?

No headline, or a weak headline, cannot capture the considerably larger numbers of customers who *would* buy from you if your headline appeal caught their interest.

How To Create a Winning Headline For Your Product or Service

I always aim to write *one hundred* different headlines for the same product. From those, I'll choose the four, five, or six I think are the best, most attention-grabbing, compelling, and targeted. Why come up with one hundred if I only want up to six? Because the more ways you can dream up of describing the benefits of your product or service, the greater chance you have of finding the *one way* that will pull the highest response.

Why do I want five or six different headlines for the same product or service? Because one headline appeal can out-pull another by **massive** margins. One headline can out-pull another by 50 - 500 percent, or more. It can mean the difference between marginal profit and runaway success.

When you find the sales appeal that attracts more customers than any other appeal, by testing one headline against others, you can multiply your sales by enormous margins without increasing your marketing budget. Why be happy accepting a small return from your pound when the same pound can generate a return many times higher?

One company changed the headline of an already profitable advertisement and received **2,100 percent more response** — 21 times more sales from the same advert at the same cost.

That's the power of headlines.

4 Tips For Creating Winning Headlines

1. Aim to write **one hundred different headlines** presenting your offer in the most attention-getting, compelling, interesting manner possible.

2.   Concentrate on the **real benefits** of your offer. Remember, all your customers are interested in is, *"What's in it for me?"*

3.   Select four, five or six of the most powerful headlines you've written.

4.   Test each headline separately. Track the response each one produces. One of your headlines will out-pull the others. Use that headline in your offers and make it your 'control' until you find a better headline that beats it. Then use that headline as your 'control,' etc. (See Chapter 18: Test And Market The Clear Winner.)

Four Headlines That Increased Response Up To 1,800 Percent

Some years ago I had a client in the dry cleaning business. He was already successful but wanted to increase his sales still further. He'd been trying to market additional related services by handing out leaflets to customers as they collected their dry-cleaning. One of the offers was for the clothes protection treatment, Scotchgard™ .

I suggested that instead of just handing out institutional-type leaflets with their company name at the top and a *me message,* they would get more response by writing to their customers direct with a benefit-oriented appeal. I wrote the offer in letter format with the headline:

> **Never Let Milk, Coffee or Gravy Stain Your Clothes Again... <u>Here's how you can protect your clothes from nasty stains... FREE!</u>**

The headline that helped pull 1,800 times more response for a Dry Cleaning business

What was the result? Their response increased from 0.4% to 7.2% — 1,800 percent more response. Do you think if you had received this letter from your dry cleaners you'd be *more likely* to read it than if it just showed the name of the company at the top? Even if it had the word Scotchgard™ across the top it doesn't tell you anything compelling about the offer.

The much increased response was made possible because protecting your clothes was brought *alive* in the headline.

Another client owned a secretarial training school. She ran small, weekly ads in her local paper with the name of her school at the top, a list of the courses she provided, her telephone number and address. The ads weren't producing a profitable response.

I rewrote her ad with the headline:

Why Some Secretaries Almost Always Get a Well Paid Job

The headline that attracted 400 percent more response for a Secretarial School

This headline pulled over **400 percent more response.** It took me one hour to write the headline and body copy in the same size ad space. It didn't cost a penny more to publish. Yet my client received 400 times more response.

That's not all. If her conversion rate from inquiry to sale remains the same, and because her premises and training terminal costs remain fixed, her profits will increase geometrically with the 400 percent increase in sales.

Three years ago I had a client in the wholesale fashion business. He sold chic, high-fashion outfits for nightclubbers and party-goers to fashion retailers throughout the country. In an effort to get additional stores to stock his garments he was sending them an information pack, a business-type letter with his company name at the top, and an opening paragraph saying, "I would like to introduce you to our new range of Paris fashion."

His letter produced a 0.6 percent response which made him a worthwhile profit.

I redesigned the package, adding a six-page, full colour brochure, a response form, and a reply-paid envelope. But the crux of the mailer was a four page letter with the headline:

<u>Before</u> you read about a Nationally featured, fast-selling fashion offer I'd like <u>your shop</u> to participate in... have a cup of tea on me!

The new headline that helped multiply response by four times for a fashion wholesaler.

Attached to the top right-hand corner of the letter was a high quality tea bag. If you owned a fashion store and a package with this headline and a tea bag arrived in your morning post, how could you ignore it?

This headline out-pulled any other I tested against it by an incredible *four to one.* The pack as a whole earned the company 2.4 million pounds extra sales at a cost of just £2,800 for printing and mailing.

Another client, Big Apple Hair and Beauty, wanted to boost the beauty side of the business. Although they offered beauty therapy to their hairdressing clients, it wasn't producing any profits. Cheryl, the owner, was becoming frustrated with the lack of response.

I suggested she send a letter to staff members of neighbouring companies, with a persuasive offer of beauty therapy. I wrote the letter and it was given to over five hundred staff. Seven weeks later it had produced a 22 percent response — over 110 staff responded. Here's the headline I used:

> ## Important Announcement to all (company) Staff... Here's a Special Treat for all Your Hard Work...

The headline that produced 22 percent response for a hair and beauty business

How To Find Compelling Headline Ideas

Whatever it is you sell, start writing headlines that you think will attract the attention of your prospective customers in the most compelling way.

When you are writing headlines think of as many specific **benefits** your product or service provides. Look at what you sell from your *customer's* point of view, not yours.

Here's a guide to the most sought-after benefits people look for when buying a product or service. Try and match *your* offer to one or more of them.

The Instant Benefit Finder

- How is it going to **help** them?
- How is it going to make their life **easier?**
- How is it going to **simplify** their life?
- How is it going to make things happen **faster** for them?
- How is it going to make things more **effective** for them?

- Is it going to help them **make more money?**
- Is it going to help them **save more money?**
- Is it going to help them get a **promotion?**
- Is it going enable them to **learn new skills?**

- Is it going to help them become **more successful?**
- Is it going to help them become **successful faster?**
- Is it going to help **satisfy their ego?**

- Is it going to help boost their **standing in society?**

- Is it going to help them retain or regain a **youthful appearance?**
- Is it going to help them become **healthier?**
- Is it going to help them become **fitter?**
- Is it going to help them **reduce weight?**

- How is it going to help them **maximise their time?**
- How is it going to help them **save time?**
- How is it going to help them make a **task easier?**
- How is it going to help them make **work more enjoyable?**
- How is it going to help them make **play more fun?**

Search for the specific benefits your product or service provides. You want to find every obvious, and not-so-obvious benefit. Then translate each individual benefit into as many different headlines as you can. With fifty, or seventy-five, or one hundred headlines to select from you have a good chance of finding the **one** that will impact your readers, listeners, or viewers most powerfully.

TIP:
Don't try to be clever, sarcastic, humorous, or salesy in your headlines (or any of your marketing). It doesn't work. Why? Because what *you* think is clever, humorous, or inventive salesmanship other people could see as awkward, humourless, or delusive.

Money spending is a serious process for customers. Don't imagine you'll attract more custom by being anything but serious and respectful.

Rather, give people interesting facts and specific information. Many more people respond to a tell-it-as-it-is approach, than one that is too stylised.

Make everything you do interesting, compelling, powerful, and exciting—but **believable** and **factual.** You'll get more response.

16 Proven Response-Words That Will Increase The Power Of Your Headlines

Certain words evoke interest more than others. When you first see them you might think they are tired, over-used cliches which people wouldn't respond to today. Don't make that mistake.

These response-words I have listed work as effectively today as they did thirty years ago. What you might think of as tired cliches are actually unskilful *uses* of particular words and phrases. Talentless copywriters assume that if they arbitrarily fill copy with as many response-words as possible, customers are bound to respond. Not so.

As with any tool of the trade, the words and phrases I am sharing with you need to be used selectively and thoughtfully.

When you use them intelligently to add power to a headline (or body copy) you'll add tremendous impact to your sales message.

Here they are:

Word 1:   "Here is," or "Here's"
For example, "Here's the Larger Computer Desk You've Been Looking For."

Word 2:   "Now"
For example, "Now You Can Feel Twice The Warmth For The Same Low Cost."

Word 3:   "New"
For example, "New CD Player Lets You Record CD's Too!"

Word 4:   "Announcing"
For example, "Announcing a New Investment Account That Gives You a Guaranteed 9% per Year."

Word 5:   "This"
For example, "This New Dishwasher Will Even Clean

Plates <u>You'd</u> Have to Soak for an Hour."

Word 6: "Why"
For example, "Why Some Secretaries Almost Always Get a Well Paid Job."

Word 7: "Advice"
For example, "Advice if You're Buying Your First PC."

Word 8: "How To"
For example, "How To Double Your Profits in Just 12 Months."

Word 9: "At Last"
For Example, "At Last... a Real and Permanent Solution To Baldness."

Word 10: "Who Else?"
For example, "Who Else Wants To Earn £51,000 This Year?"

Word 11: "Powerful"
For example, "Powerful New PC Works Faster Than Any Other Computer."

Word 12: "Wanted"
For example, "Wanted — Seven Homes That Need a New Driveway Before Christmas."

Word 13: "Which"
For example, "Which One of These Business Suits Would You Choose To Wear?"

Word 14: "Amazing"
For example, "Amazing Eye Sight Discovery Corrects Short Sight in One Hour."

Word 15: "You" or "Your"
For example, "Your Skin Will Look and Feel Smoother

Than It Ever Has in Just 7 Days."

Word 16: "Incredible"
For example, "Incredible New Engine Does
97 Miles to the Gallon."

21 Attention-Grabbing Headlines

Here are 21 examples of how you can create powerful headlines for any product or service. As you read them they should spark plenty of ideas of how you can create winning headlines for what you sell.

Headline #1: An offer from a kitchen and bathroom manufacturer to builders:

> **Attention all Builders... You Can Now Earn**
> **£5,370+ Extra Cash Than Last Year When**
> **You Fit a Shefferd Kitchen or Bathroom**

Headline #2: A window display design company selling their services to store owners:

> **How To Attract Hundreds More Customers**
> **Into Your Store With a Powerful Window Display**

Headline #3: An electricity suppliers method of attracting new customers:

> **7 Quick Ways To Reduce Your Heating Bill**
> **This Year**

Headline #4: A family car:

> **This New 5-Seat Family Saloon Offers More**
> **Comfort, Safety, and Accessories Than Any**
> **Other Car in its Category**

Headline #5: A wardrobe, selling on price:

This Solid Pine Wardrobe Has More Space and Facilities Than Any Other Wardrobe at its Price

Headline #6: A wardrobe, selling on flexibility:

This Wardrobe Changes To Fit Your Needs. More Shelf Space, or More Hanging Space... It Adjusts in Minutes

Headline #7: A diet method:

The Day She <u>Stopped</u> Dieting, The Pounds Started Falling Off

Headline #8: A vacuum cleaner:

Suck-Up More Dust, Dirt, Mites and Bugs With The Amazing Bugsucker... The Most Powerful Vacuum on Earth

Headline #9: Hi-Fi Store:

If You Are Buying a New Hi Fi This Week, You <u>Must</u> Read This Important Message

Headline #10: Computer service company:

Most Computer Service Companies Take up to 8 Hours To Get To You. We Guarantee To Take a MAXIMUM of One Hour To Get To Your Door

Headline #11: A stain remover:

If Your Carpet Has a Stubborn Wine, Coffee, or Mud Stain, New Instant-Acting *Stain Dissolver*

Will Wipe it Away in Seconds

Headline #12: A men's clothing store:

Looking For a £65 Shirt for Just £29? We've Got 257 in Stock This Saturday... But Hurry

Headline #13: A men's suit store:

If You're Looking For a Smart Pure Wool Suit, We Have 207 For Sale at a Price You Won't Beat

Headline #14: A suite store:

The New Bentley 3-Piece Suite Gives You a Lifetime of Luxurious Comfort and Support, Contoured To Relax Your Limbs and Support Your Back

Headline #15: An up-market health spa

Here's a Special Invitation To Spend an Invigorating Morning at the Luxurious Roman Bath Health Spa For Just £10

Headline #16: A restaurant:

Dine at The Fabulous French Riviera Restaurant For Just £5 Each with this Introductory Invitation

Headline #17: An up-market service garage:

Does Your Mercedes, Lexus, or BMW Need Maintenance? I'll Maintain Your Saloon With Factory-Trained Specialists To The Highest Demanded Standard, 24-Hours a Day

Headline #18: A holiday company:

> **Take a First-Class Trip to the Stunning
> Island of Fiji — Now, You Can Afford
> To Bring The Family Too**

Headline #19: A fax machine:

> **This Fax Will Speed Your Message Anywhere
> in the World at an Incredible 10 Pages a Minute**

Headline #20: A loudspeaker manufacturer:

> **For The Size of a Can of Soup, These Astonishing
> New Speakers Sound as Clear, Full, and Powerful
> as a Rock Concert at The Albert Hall**

Headline #21: A cosmetic product:

> **New Collagen Breakthrough Leaves Your Skin
> Clearer, Tighter and More Youthful in Just
> 10 Days**

Make Your Headlines Specific

Headlines work most effectively when they are specific. **Specifics always out-sell generalities.**

If I said, *Your skin will quickly become more youthful-looking* it doesn't convince you as much as if I quoted a specific time period: *Your skin will become more youthful-looking in just 10 days.*

The specific element quickly makes the statement more believable.

This petrol additive will give you more miles to the gallon is not as powerful as, *This petrol additive will give you 7 more miles to every gallon of petrol.*

Always be specific in your headlines (and your body copy).

Remember though, that headlines are your most powerful

tool for attracting maximum numbers of customers. Always be honest and ethical in describing your offer.

As long as your cosmetic cream really *will* make customer's skin look more youthful in 10 days, and as long as your petrol additive really *does* produce 7 extra miles to every gallon, you're perfectly entitled to say so. But never exaggerate your claims. They will only backfire on you.

If you write a great headline that increases your response dramatically, but your claim is false, your effort is wasted.

You do not have to consider exaggerating your claims when you can quite easily create winning headlines honestly and ethically.

Work within the parameters of your product or service, but certainly find the most persuasive way of describing it!

Turn to the Chapter 6 to learn: **How To Keep Customers Riveted To Your Sales Message...**

CHAPTER 6

How To Keep Customers Riveted To Your Sales Message

A few years ago I went with some friends to an all-day concert at Wembley stadium in London. 70,000 fans packed the stadium waiting for the act to begin.

Suddenly, the stage lights came on, dry ice plumed off the stage, the crowd roared in expectation, and.... **nothing!** It was a false start!

That's how many adverts, sales letters, brochures, and other sales messages perform. They grab the attention of prospects with a good headline promise. But the promise turns out to be false or misleading. Or the sales story that follows it does not *follow through* on the promise that caught prospects attention, or it is *boring,* or it does not quickly *grip the reader* with persuasive benefits and promises of betterment.

After you've attracted your prospective customer's attention with a powerful headline, you've got to *keep* him or her reading, listening, or watching your sales message.

If you fail — if you 'disappoint' your prospects by not quickly keeping them interested in your offer — they will abandon your message.

Use This 7-Step Formula

There is a 7-step formula for leading your prospect from being initially attracted by your headline, to buying your product or service.

Use the formula in full when you have space to explain your offer in *detail* — full page space ads, sales letters, and brochures.

Give your prospects as much interesting information about your offer as you can. The more detail and interesting, specific information you provide the more response you'll get.

But, I hear you say, shouldn't you keep your sales message short and to the point? Surely customers don't want to read a ton of information? Or do they?

This is one of the most misunderstood areas of marketing. At my seminars, business owners always ask this same question. The fact is, **the more you tell, the more you sell.** Always explain your offer in full, interesting detail. Don't cut it short. When you tell the full sales story **many more customers will buy your product.** (See Chapter 7: Explain What You Sell In *Detail.*)

Here are the 7-steps to keeping your prospects and customers riveted to your sales message:

1.   Create a powerful, benefit-oriented headline.

2.   Immediately follow through with the promise made in the headline.

3.   Tell prospects specifically what they are going to get.

4.   Back up your claims with proof and endorsements.

5.   Tell your prospects what they will lose if they don't act.

6.   Rephrase your most important benefits in your closing offer.

7.   Ask for action. Now.

Here's how to incorporate each step in your offer. Let's say you are a car manufacturer. You have developed a family saloon with new standards of impact protection. You are aiming at family buyers who put safety first. You're designing a full page ad for a national newspaper.

Here's how you could approach each of the 7 steps:

Step 1: Your headline

Let's assume you've written the headline:

"You are <u>safer</u> in the new 5-seat SI700 than in any other car in its category"

Step 2: Immediately follow through with the promise made in your headline.

Your headline has attracted targeted prospective buyers who want *safety* first. An effective way to lead them into the rest of your sales message is to quickly expand on the promise made in your headline with a sub-headline.

Car buyers who list safety as their main concern are not without vanity. They are almost certainly interested in comfort and accessories too. So to keep your prospect hooked you could say:

If you need the space and comfort a luxury family saloon offers, but you also want to know your passengers are uniquely protected against even a hard impact, the new SI700 will interest you.

Then you could start your body copy like this:

What's more, you'll enjoy a level of comfort usually only associated with saloons costing twice the price. Plus you have 27 advanced interior and exterior driving functions electronically controlled at the push of a button to make your drive even more comfortable — and safe.

You've hooked your prospect's interest, haven't you? You've provided more detailed information based on the promise in your headline. Then:

Step 3: Tell your prospects specifically what they are going to get.

Example: **When it comes to keeping your family safe in the** event of an accident, you want to know no short-cuts have been taken. When the SI700 was on the drawing board, the instruction to our design engineers was, "Build a car that is stronger and safer than anything on the road." It took them 5 years and 6 weeks to achieve, but the results have set high new standards for the motor industry.

The entire engine and boot compartments are built around a web of solid steel bars that will take an impact of up to 56 miles an hour without distorting the passenger cabin even 1 inch.

The SI700's four doors are fortified against impact with the unique LifeProtect System™ developed by our engineers. A formidably strong 'H' shaped steel guard in each door locks tight into the door frame when closed to protect you against a side impact of up to 48 miles an hour.

Inside the protected passenger cabin, four airbags are fitted — two in the front, and two stowed in the back of the front seats for your rear passengers.

If this saloon had been available a year ago in England 3,867 serious road injuries could have been avoided. That's the number of passengers injured because their cars did *not* meet our new, record-high impact standard.

As you can see, we take your safety as seriously as our own.

You might think that a car so focused on safety would lack in comfort and stylish accessories. Not so. When you first sit in an SI700, you'll be surprised by its luxurious feel and sophisticated styling.

Every seat in the cabin supports and secures you and your passengers. But the seats are much more than *just* seats. In the depth of winter you can heat each seat individually to between 20 - 50 degrees. In the heat of summer, each seat can be air cooled to maximise your comfort.

And — unlike most of our competitors — we do not think one

seat fits all. Individual, electronic seat adjustment at the flick of a switch allows you to shape the seat to suit your posture. Not only that, but you can enter your personal adjustment into the seat's memory. Next time you get in the SI700, if someone else has adjusted your seat differently, simply punch the memory pad, and the seat will readjust to your position.

Do you see how the *detail* and *specifics* make the sales message *interesting?*

Now you have to:

Step 4: Back up your claims with proof and endorsements.

If your product is stronger, faster, slower to deteriorate, longer lasting, more comfortable, more effective, safer, or whatever, unless you back up your claim with proof people won't believe you, and therefore will not respond.

Endorsements are an effective way to prove what you claim is true. **But not all endorsements work.**

How many times have you read a list of endorsements for an offer that do not do anything to motivate you to buy it? To increase your desire to buy, an endorsement must cite *circumstantial results*. It must tell you of an *actual result gained*.

Here are the two types of endorsement; the type that has little buying persuasion and which you should avoid in your marketing, and the type that will substantially increase your prospects motivation to buy.

Superlative. This is the type found in most sales messages, but they fail to influence or persuade a person to buy. Superlative quotes include:

"I have just received your information pack. I am very impressed and can't wait to get started!"

"The suit I bought from you looks great on me. Thank you."

"I am really pleased with the PC. I have just set it up and it looks much more professional than my old one!"

These types of endorsement only leave your prospects thinking *so what?* They don't tell you anything specific. They are bland, empty statements, and a waste of your marketing space.

Anecdotal. This is the type that quotes an **actual** experience, history, event, before-and-after story, circumstance, or result gained. People can *relate* to actual events experienced by others, so the endorsement strikes home.

The more you can induce your prospects to 'feel' and 'experience' what you are selling prior to owning it, the more readily they will buy. Anecdotal endorsements have a powerful touch-and-feel factor. They *involve* your prospect in a real-life advantage gained by your product or service.

Here's a persuasive anecdotal endorsement for a car dealership:

"I was astonished at the service John Smith Dealership gave me when my 14 month old 300LE broke down on the motorway last month. They reached me within 25-minutes of my call, towed me home, then took the car away to find out what had gone wrong.

That same afternoon they phoned me and explained the engine had blown, and that they were extremely sorry for the inconvenience it had caused me. Fifteen minutes later they had delivered a courtesy car for me to use. Three days later they returned my car with a brand new engine fitted free of charge.

I will always buy my cars from John Smith because he really cares about his customers."

Do you think this actual-experience endorsement is more persuasive than an empty superlative quote like, *"I have always been very impressed with John Smith's after sales service?"* You bet!

Nearly every driver can relate to breaking down at the most inconvenient time. So the story of John Smith's superb service creates a powerful, persuasive endorsement. The *detail* of this customer's experience makes the endorsement compelling.

Four Sources of Endorsements That Work More Persuasively

1. Endorsements from other people or businesses that have bought your product *and have gained advantage from it.*

2. Endorsements from recognised authority figures within your industry.

3. Endorsements from professionals.

4. Quotes from reviews and editorials about your product or service from well respected national publications, and publications within your industry.

In your SI700 car marketing, you could add proof and endorsements like this:

It might be said we could be over-enthusiastic about the higher than normal impact protection we've achieved. So to make sure we weren't biased, we took the SI700 along to the Motoring Association for an independent view.

Here's what their Chief Safety Engineer said.

"The patented 'H' steel crash bars in every door are a breakthrough in impact protection. We ran five separate side collision tests, and sure enough, in every test the SI700 withstood an impact of up to 48 miles per hour. Any passengers in the car during the impact would have survived unscathed."

Other independent sources are astonished at the SI700's safety, too.

Motoring magazine classes the SI700 as, "Extraordinarily safe. There is no other car in its category that will protect you against forceful impact so effectively." Nov 1997.

"Our crash tests revealed the new SI700 to be the safest family saloon on the road." *Consumer,* **Jan 1998.**

"I have just gone and bought an SI700 for my wife. Life is too precious to risk destroying in a road accident. The SI700's new safety standards mean I can sleep sounder knowing my wife and family are better protected." **Senior Surgeon, Accident & Emergency Department, London Hospital.**

Step 5: Tell your prospects what they will lose if they don't act.

It stands to reason that if your prospect does not buy your product he will lose out on the benefit or advantage it offers. Tell your prospect what he will lose.

Or will he lose a *different* opportunity like a limited time offer, or a reduced price, or a bundle offer, or a free bonus or extended guarantee? Point it out to him.

If you don't choose the SI700, will you ever feel quite as safe driving? Really, when it comes to safety, there is now no other choice. You and your family will simply not be as safe in any other car. By a life-saving 43 percent.

Step 6: Rephrase your most important benefits in your closing offer

Now you want to encapsulate the essence of your offer. Remind your prospects of the main benefits of your product. This is a powerful prelude to asking for action. You can intensify your prospect's desire to own the product by summing up its benefits here.

The more benefits your prospect can recall, the easier it is for him or her to justify buying your product.

In a nutshell, if you are looking for uncompromising safety, in a saloon luxuriously designed for a silent, comfortable driving experience, plus a myriad of additional electronically con-

trolled features normally only found in a car costing twice as much, the new SI700 cannot be compared.

I think you'll also agree the stylish body design does everything to visually impress while effectively disguising the fortress within.

Step 7: Ask for action. Now.

One of the biggest marketing mistakes I see companies make is failing to effectively **ask for action.**

I see full-page national newspaper ads that cost anything up to £70,000 with no effective call to action. I see sales letters from well known national companies using no effective call to action. I see television ads that have cost hundreds of thousands of pounds using no effective call to action.

If you fail to use an effective call to action at the end of your advert, sales letter, mailer, etc., you are wasting a large proportion of the cash resources you've invested in it.

Why? Because if you do not motivate people into taking some form of action, large numbers will **not** act.

Most marketing fails to effectively motivate prospects to respond. Substantial additional sales that could readily be garnered from existing ads, sales letters, brochures, etc. are lost because no effective call to action is employed.

If you specifically ask your prospect to take the precise action you want him or her to take, your sales will multiply considerably.

Why Most Advertisers Lose The Bigger Response They Could Easily Receive

Advertising is probably the most misunderstood form of marketing. Most companies—and regrettably, most advertising agencies—assume that if you simply 'show' a product in a creative, glitzy way, customers will rush to buy it.

Look at TV commercials. A product is shown in a gloriously glossy, creative — *expensive* — film piece that espouses the supposed lifestyle benefits you'll gain if you own it. Almost never are you given specific, compelling, persuasive benefits. Hardly ever will you see an advertisement asking the viewer to **take action** to **sample** or **buy** the product **now.**

Every good salesperson knows it's not enough to simply 'present' your product. You've got to ask for an order to win a sale. *Advertising is nothing less than salesmanship.*

If more advertisers understood the importance of the 7- step process of motivating customers to buy — particularly asking for action — millions of pounds would be saved on ineffective and inefficient advertising. Advertisers allow large groups of prospective customers to fall through their net because their marketing messages fail to lead the customer to take the final step — **respond!**

The very *least* you want *your* prospect to do is pick up the telephone and call for more information, send for a free sample, arrange a test, or fix an appointment.

Even better, if it's appropriate, you want your prospect to **buy** from you now.

Here are six types of effective call to action you can use:

1. Telephone, write, or fax for further information.

2. Ask for a free sample.

3. Ask for a demonstration or test, at home, work, in a store, or at your site.

4. Ask for a 30-day free, no obligation trial.

5. Ask your prospect to visit a store and buy or receive a *sample* product.

6. Motivate your prospect to visit a store and buy a *full* product.

Motivate your prospect to *do something*. If you don't, you've lost their immediate attention and you will have to start the whole process over again to recapture that person's interest.

In short, you have only **one chance** to take hold of your prospect's hand, and lead him or her through the selling process right to the stage of buying your product. That chance is created **at the point** of advertising, not sometime **after** the point of advertising.

Here's an example of how you could ask for action in your car ad:

Find out for yourself how safe—and luxuriously comfortable—the SI700 is. Simply CALL Freephone 0800 111 2234 to arrange a test drive at your nearest dealer.

Alternatively, ask us to send you the full colour brochure, "Why the SI700 is the safest, most luxurious saloon on the road," plus the Automobile Organisation's special report on the 7 safest saloons on the market.

Detail sells! Turn to Chapter 7 to discover how to double your sales, or more, by providing your customers with interesting detail about your product or service...

CHAPTER 7

Explain What You Sell
in *Detail*

Traditional marketing advice says *keep your sales message short. People don't want to read stacks of information about your product. They haven't got the time. Nor are they interested.*

But this is erroneous. **The very opposite is true.**

You should tell as much as you can about your product, in every piece of marketing you put out.

Think when you last bought a product. Isn't it true you were interested in knowing as much about it as possible?

If you were interested in buying a new stereo system you wouldn't just walk into the nearest store and buy one right off the shelf. You would want to know something about it. Is it in your price bracket? What power is it? Will it play clearly with accurate sound reproduction? Will it play cassette tapes as well as CD's? Has it got a tuner? What tone adjustments does it have? Is it a reliable make? Will it look good in my sitting room? There are *many* questions you want answers to before you can make a buying decision.

Customers **like** and **need** to have information about what they are buying because they are **interested** and want to be **informed and educated** before they purchase.

Additionally, the more **interesting, factual information** a customer discovers about your offer, the **better-value** they perceive it to be.

The Psychology of Buying—Understand This And You Understand Your Customer

The higher the price ticket, the more a customer goes through a series of judgemental, justificational, and emotional decision-making before he or she buys.

First: A customer has to be in the market for a product or service like yours. Much marketing wastes pounds because it attempts to interest people who are not interested or have no need for the offer. Contrary to some belief, 'everyone' is **not** your potential market, even if you have an everyday product. Your 'universe' consists only of prospects who are *in the market* for your type of product.

Your prospect first **sees** your print or TV ad, sales letter, insert, flyer, or **hears** your radio ad, telemarketing call, or salesperson and decides whether it is a relevant message, or it is not.

Second: Your prospect **judges** your offer. Does it provide the benefits he or she wants, needs, desires, craves after, aspires to? Is it the right size, shape, weight, texture, quality? Is it in a price band your prospect is comfortable paying? How does it compare in value with competing products or services?

Third: Many people buy on an **emotional** basis. The higher the ticket price, or the more of a luxury your product is, the more emotion is involved in your customer's buying decision.

If your product or service is a necessity—like a liquid to unblock your drain, petrol for your car, a new pane of glass to replace a broken window, etc.—emotion has less to do with the buying decision. (Although, even with necessities, when your customer has a choice of competing products or services, or competing outlets, emotion often swings the sale. You could want the drain cleaner with the **strongest** packaging on the shelf because you feel it will work more powerfully; you could decide to buy your petrol from the **cleanest** petrol station in the neighborhood; you could decide to buy your replacement glass from the **friendliest** glazier.) Emotional buying effects nearly **all** purchases by some degree.

But let's say a man, John, was a mid-income earner, his car was old, and although he didn't actually *need* to replace it yet and could do with spending his money on more sensible needs around the house, he had his heart set on owning a brand new BMW 3-Series. One day John sees a great deal—a new 3-Series in his favourite colour, racing red, with a great finance deal that he could just about afford. He falls in love with the car. He imagines how impressed his friends will be, how his drinking buddies will all ask to have a drive, how his colleagues at work will look at him with envy.

Emotion is a powerful force. John **really wants** that car! He *sees* himself driving it. Because his emotions begin to rule, he'll come up with all the reasons on earth why buying it is actually a *sensible* thing to do. He will look to *justify* his urge to buy. The more you satisfy John's need for justification in your marketing, the more you will help him make his buying decision.

The same applies to most 'luxury' items. Customers want to, and have to be able to, justify buying the product or service they *want* to own.

Fourth: The need to **justify** a purchase extends beyond the customer himself. The buyer often has to justify the purchase to **other people**—family, friends, colleagues, club members—in order to feel good about the purchase him or herself. John might say to his wife, "I know it's a little bit more expensive than an average car,"—it may really be 50 percent more than a sensible car for John's circumstances—"but it's construction quality means it will last years longer than a cheaper car, so it's a good investment in the long run."

You'll justify buying a £400 suit when it would be more sensible to buy a £200 suit and put the extra £200 towards a new shed, by convincing yourself the suit will look more impressive in front of your clients and therefore help you win more sales.

You also might have to justify it to your wife, or husband. They are onto you to buy that new shed. The old one is falling down! So you have to persuade your spouse that the expensive suit will be good for business. You persuade by *justifying* the purchase—making it seem a smart decision.

Children Are Experts at Justifying Why They Should Get What They Want—Listen To Them!

I learn from my three year old niece, Lauren, every time I see her. She's smart. In her three short years, she's figured that adults are always busy doing something important when she wants to play. She's realised the difference between 'wanting' and 'needing' something. She doesn't always get what she **wants.** But when she **needs** something, adults have to listen.

When Joanie and I were visiting last Christmas, she came up to me and said, "Uncle Paul, I need you to help me build a truck with the building blocks."

Being clever, because we adults were right in the middle of watching a good movie, I said, "But you're really good at building a truck with the blocks. You go and build one, and I'll come and look at it in a minute."

"But I *need* you to help me," she said, quickly thinking how to persuade me, "because I can't build a truck without you."

How could I refuse? Talk about effective justification. Lauren is an expert. You think she'll lose her ability as an adult? I doubt it. Watch out for Lauren!

The More You Tell, The More You Sell

The more you **tell** about your product or service, the more you **sell.** Can you see why? The more your prospective customer learns about your offer, the more he or she can **judge** its suitability, become **emotionally attached** to it, and be able to **justify** buying it.

If all I tell you is that the racing red BMW is a good car, you haven't got much to go on.

But if I tell you it is a good car because it is mechanically superior than its competitors, the engine will usually last 55,000 miles longer than average, that it has safer road holding, and that its resale value remains higher than most cars in its category, you have a lot more information to go on.

Long Sales Letters Invariably Outsell Short Letters

Most businesses send out short, one or two-page sales letters. Traditional marketing advice teaches that letters *should* be short and to the point. But a letter is simply salesmanship in print. **Would you expect to win sales if your salesperson was short and to the point?** Of course you wouldn't.

I've seen two page sales letters outsell one page for the same product. I've seen four pages outsell two, eight pages outsell four, sixteen pages outsell eight — even 24 pages outsell 16, and 32 pages outsell 24.

I'll show you in detail how to write sales letters that sell, in Chapter 13. But for now, realise that ninety-nine times out of a hundred the more you tell, the more you sell, no matter what medium you're selling in.

You cannot make your sales message too long. Only too *boring*. If your prospect is interested in what you are offering, he or she will read as much appealing, absorbing, and engrossing information as you provide.

A well informed prospect is a prospect ready to buy. If you provide more compelling, interesting, and persuasive information than your competitors, you'll outsell every one. Your sales will skyrocket when you tell more.

How a Client Increased Her Response 3050% By Telling More

The hair and beauty salon owner I told you about earlier used to run small institutional ads that typically produced two or three responses a week.

I rewrote her ad with the headline **100 HAIRCUTS for just £2 each by professional stylist** and told *as much as I possibly could* about the offer in the allotted space. The new ad pulled 61 responses in three days — a 3050 percent increase. Same size ad. Same newspaper. Same page position. But **3050 percent more response.** That's the power of telling more.

Had I *not* told as much about the offer, and not given the reason for the £2 hair cuts, the ad would not have succeeded.

How This Shoe Store Outsells Its Competitors

Joanie and I spent this Christmas in San Diego, California, with her family. One day we decided to spend an afternoon shopping in the glorious 75-degree sunshine. Amongst other things we both wanted, I needed a pair of new dress shoes.

After searching four or five shoe stores, we came across a Johnston & Murphy store, that presented itself very differently. This store took the trouble to *explain* how their shoes are made, the quality of the leathers, the reason why they are more comfortable and shock-absorbing, and why they will last for years.

They have a beautifully illustrated colour brochure with every shoe and style available, packed with interesting and informative descriptions next to each photograph. They even provided cross-section diagrams of their shoes showing how each one is made for comfort and allows your foot to breath.

The perceived value of a Johnston & Murphy shoe is that of greater value for the dollar than others in their price range.

Does this persuade me to buy their shoes? You bet. Will I be sufficiently impressed to tell my friends and colleagues? Well, I am telling **you** already! When you give as much interesting information about your product or service as you can, prospects will perceive you as providing more value, and your sales will multiply.

How To Make Your Marketing Bristle With Persuasive Sales Power

Remember, you cannot provide too much interesting information. Marketing that does **not** respond well isn't too long. It's just too boring, or has too much sales hype. The secret to writing sales copy that bristles with persuasive selling power is: **Make your sales message interesting, informative, newsworthy, helpful, and educational.**

Turn the page to discover how to: **Generate Higher Response By Giving Your *Reasons-Why...***

CHAPTER 8

Generate Higher Response by Giving Your *Reasons-Why*

Many sales messages don't produce the higher response they could because they fail to include a *reason why*.

Why should customers buy from you instead of your competitor? **Why** is your product or service superior? **Why** is your product smaller, bigger, quieter, more comfortable, more firm, more refined, tastier, luxurious, longer-lasting?

Why is your price lower? **Why** is your price higher? **Why** do you supply it in 18 colours? **Why** do you only supply it in black, red, and blue? **Why** is your location more convenient? **Why? Why? Why?**

Whenever you put out any sales message, if you do not include a reason-why it is simply a superlative, bland statement. It has no believable or persuasive substance. In effect you are saying, *"Here's my offer, I know it sounds almost too good to be true but I haven't got time or space to explain it fully, so just trust me and buy it!"*

Would **you** buy a product or service on a just-trust-me-and-see basis? No, of course you wouldn't. Yet every month I see hundreds of sales messages that fail to produce much more than a meagre response because the *reason-why* is not explained.

How This Blind Manufacturer Sold His Entire Overstock in 8-Days

I have a client who manufactures beautiful roller and Venetian blinds for use at home. One day he called me and said, "Paul, I've found myself with an overstock of 15,000 metres of material. I need to sell it quickly in order to make space for new stock arriving in three weeks. For two months I've been trying to sell it at 50 percent off but it's not budging. I'll lose too much money if I have to throw it out. What can I do?"

I explained how he could sell his material quite quickly. He looked dubious, but because he'd already been trying for two months without success, he accepted it and went off. Eight days later he called me back. He'd sold the entire overstock, fully recovered his costs, and picked up a number of profitable new orders at the same time.

Here's The Secret

What was my secret? I simply explained the **reasons-why**. We told customers *why* the blinds were being sold at half price, and *why* if they wanted to buy they had to purchase quickly. I just *told the truth*. Basically, this is what I wrote to his customers:

"Dear Customer,

I wouldn't normally write to you like this, but I have an embarrassing problem that could turn out to be your gain.

I have just discovered I am holding an overstock of material for roller and Venetian blinds that is taking up space I need for new stock that is arriving in three weeks.

As you know my blinds are not the cheapest—in fact I pride myself that they're the best you can buy. But because of my overstock, I thought it would be nice to offer my existing customers an opportunity to buy any blinds they want at a much reduced price, to help me make space in the warehouse.

Because of my now somewhat urgent problem, I am prepared to sell these blinds for **half the price** you'd normally pay.

Every blind will be made by hand with the same care and attention to detail you know I insist on.

Most importantly, **every blind will come with our usual lifetime guarantee.**

To be frank, selling at 50% means my profit is wiped out. But because you are doing me a favour helping to clear space for my next delivery, profit is less important than making space in my warehouse.

One more thing. Because the price I'm offering is rock-bottom, yet the blinds you'll receive are the very same quality and supremacy you'd normally pay twice as much for, the stock will sell quickly.

If you are keen to take advantage of my—slightly embarrassing—half price offer, I urge you to order quickly before the overstock runs out. As soon as it's gone *I cannot make this offer again.*

Call me on freephone 0800 123456 to place your order. Your hand-made blinds will be with you within 24 hours, delivered to your door."

Isn't that more believable and persuasive than a sales message that just says, **"Half price blinds sale?"** Doesn't it help allay any doubts you have about the authenticity and quality of the blinds? Doesn't it answer your first question, "Why is he selling them at half price? What's the catch?"

U.S. Experiment Shows 56 Percent More People Respond When Given a Reason-Why

An interesting experiment in the USA in 1978 confirmed that **people respond more when given a 'reason-why'.**

Social psychologist, Ellen Langer, ran a series of experiments* by asking people who were queuing to use a photocopier in a busy library if she could jump the queue and do some photocopying herself.

The words she used were, **"Excuse me, I have five pages. May I use the photocopier?"** 60 percent of the people she asked agreed to her request.

She then repeated the experiment, but this time added a *reason-why* she wanted to jump the queue. She asked, **"Excuse me, I have five pages. May I use the photocopier because I'm in a rush?"** The number of people who agreed to her request now jumped to 94 percent.

*Langer, Blank, & Chanowitz, 1978

She received a massive **56 percent increase** in response simply by including a reason-why in her question—*because I'm in a rush.*

Further, it was found that the single word *because* was even more important than the reason itself. The fact that you provide people with a *because* is enough for many more to respond.

Boost <u>Your</u> Sales By Up To 56 Percent, or More

Whenever you make a statement, claim, or offer related to your product, give your prospects a reason-why it is so—a 'because'.

If your exercise product burns body fat more efficiently than competing exercisers, tell your prospects why that is possible.

If you have developed an engine that will last 25 percent longer than all other engines, tell your prospects why that is possible.

If you make an ice cream that has bigger chunks than any other brand, tell your prospects why you decided to make it that way.

Why Do More People Respond To Reasons-Why?

Your customers are intelligent, interested people. They are curious, and choosy. They have a natural tendency to ask questions about what they are presented with.

The more you feed their intellect, interest, curiosity, and need with reasons-why your product is what you say it is, the more you answer their silent questions and remove their doubts. An informed and educated prospect is a prospect ready to buy.

Make Your Reasons *Believable*

If I say to you, *This Vacuum is the best you can buy because it's powerful beyond belief,* you probably won't be convinced.

But if I said, *This vacuum is the best you can buy. Why? Because it will suck up more dirt, dust and carpet mites than any other vacuum tested. 7 independent laboratory tests, including the Consumer Association's February Comparison Test, have proved the BugSucker to be the most powerful vacuum made,* it is more convincing. I have provided you with believable reasons-why.

What is the best way to make your reasons-why believable? Tell the truth! Contrary to many marketer's beliefs, customers don't respond to bucket loads of sales hype. They want the truth!

The truth about your product is much more believable, and will produce significantly higher sales than any empty sales hype.

Go to the next page to discover—**Chapter 9: My Secret Weapon...**

CHAPTER 9

My Secret Weapon...
Risk-Reversal

There is a simple, but *critical*, marketing principle and selling philosophy that you can incorporate into every sales proposition and business transaction you make, that will have such a profound effect on your sales that it's almost unfair to use against your competitors.

It is so disarmingly effective — yet simple to embrace — that I urge *all* my clients to adopt it. I urge you to do the same.

Some years ago, I was helping a friend sell business promotion and incentive products. The products were good, and together we made the business quite successful.

But one thing used to frustrate me. I would regularly come across a client who showed an enthusiastic interest in our range of products, told me, yes, the package I suggested would help to promote their business, and yes, they were very interested in buying. But they never *did* buy.

It would be too easy to justify it by thinking they weren't seriously interested in the first place. But people don't make an effort if they're not interested. There had to be a different reason.

Many businesses suffer the same problem. Many prospects inquire, or look, or sample a product. But only a few *buy*.

Why?

Here's the reason: every customer, whenever they contemplate buying *any* product or service, silently asks, "Will this *really* work for me? Is this the *best* choice I can make, or is there something better I should look for?"

Every business experiences this customer doubt and hesitation. I constantly get asked by business owners, "Why does a customer show sincere interest in my product, and then delay buying it, or not buy at all?

It is because the seller unknowingly erects a barrier between himself or herself, and the buyer.

Here's a story that explains it.

The Little Girl Buys a Puppy

A young father wanted to buy a Golden Retriever puppy for his 6-year old daughter, who'd been begging him for months, to let her have one.

He started looking at various breeders in the area, and found one that was offering an eight-week old puppy for £350.

Not knowing too much about puppies, he wanted to make sure he got a healthy, well cared for puppy from a good pedigree. If anything went wrong, if the puppy became ill, his daughter would be devastated.

So he asked the breeder a few questions. "Yes," the breeder replied, "the puppy is from a good pedigree and there are no signs of illness or health problems. Everything will be perfectly fine. *Do you want to buy the puppy?"*

Although his daughter, who had come along, was keen to take the puppy right home with her, the father wasn't sure they should rush into it. The puppy *looked* healthy, and the breeder *said* he's from a reliable pedigree, but.... not knowing much about dogs, he decided he'd rather look around a bit more. "Sweetheart," he said, "let's wait to see if there's an even prettier puppy at the next breeders."

They soon found a second breeder. He too seemed to have a bright, healthy puppy at the same price, £350.

But sensing the father's hesitation, the breeder said, "If you want to take the puppy today, I'll give you a month's worth of food to start him off properly."

The father thought that maybe he should go ahead and buy *this* puppy, especially with a month's worth of free food. But still, free food is no good if the puppy becomes sick. *I wish I knew more about dogs so that I could be sure I buy wisely* he thought.

He said to the breeder, "Let me think about it for a while."

Then, a third breeder caught his eye. When they walked in his daughter ran right over to the litter and picked up the most boisterous little hound, who started licking her face furiously. She pleaded with her father, "Daddy, please, *please,* can I take *this* one home?"

The breeder asked, "Do you know much about puppies, Sir?"

"No," the father replied, being honest. "It's difficult to know if the puppy is healthy, and won't develop any problems after we get it home. Between you and me, I also wonder if my daughter will still be as excited about him in a months time as she is today, when the novelty wears off."

"Aah," the breeder said, "then this is what I'll do for you."

"The puppy your daughter has in her arms *is* from a good pedigree. We've been breeding for eighteen years now, and all my experience tells me it is perfectly healthy."

"But I don't want you, or your daughter, to worry after you get the little boy home. Let me bring the puppy to your house by 4 o'clock this afternoon with a basket he'll be comfortable sleeping in. I'll show you how to look after him, when and how to feed him, and how to start house-training him. Also, before I bring him around, I'll have our vet check him over and issue a medical certificate to make doubly sure he starts off with a clean bill of health."

Then he went one step further. He said, *"I'll let you keep him for a month without paying me yet, to make sure your daughter still wants him after the novelty has worn off. I'll pay for all his food so you don't have any expense during the month.*

"If she still loves him as much in a month as she does today, and as long as you are happy that he is still in the very best of health, you will probably want to keep him.

"Only if you are completely happy, and if you are certain he'll bring you and your daughter the happiness you expect, just send me a cheque for £350 at the end of the month, and keep the puppy.

"But if you don't want to keep him for any reason—if you find looking after him is more work than you thought, or if your daughter doesn't find him as much fun as she thought she would, simply call me

and I'll come to collect him.

"I won't charge you a penny for the month you've had him. There'll be no hard feelings, either.

"After all, I will only be happy selling you one of my puppies if I know he's going to be loved in his new home as much as we love him here."

Now, which breeder would *you* buy the puppy from? The first, who offers you a healthy-looking puppy for £350, the second who offers you a healthy-looking puppy for £350 plus a month's worth of food, or the third who offers to let you keep the puppy for 30-days without cost, obligation, or risk?

The third, of course!

You'd be foolish not to accept the risk-free offer.

Because he realised he was taking no risk by accepting the third breeder's offer, he agreed.

Sure enough, by the end of the month, the puppy was in the best of health. In fact, he had become one of the family.

When the breeder called to ask if he should come and collect the puppy, the father said, "We couldn't be without him now for anything. I'll bring the cheque for £350 right around."

The family appreciated the breeders way of doing business—allowing them to buy the puppy without any risk.

The breeder was happy; he made the sale, and gained a very satisfied customer.

The two other breeders remained puzzled over why the nice father and daughter who seemed so interested in buying a puppy never came back.

In Most Selling Situations The Customer Is Asked To Bear The Risk

Whenever two or more people come together in any form of transaction, one side is always asked to bear the risk. In most selling transactions it is the *customer* who shoulders the risk. This is a big mistake. It is also a gross injustice to the customer.

Why? Because it is rare that your prospective customer is

familiar with and can therefore trust your product or service like you can. You are familiar with its benefits, *and* shortcomings. You know the value of what you sell.

But your customer *does not.*

The one burning question every customer has before they buy is: "Will this really work for me? Will it really do what it *promises* to do?"

The more you appease these doubts, and the more you do to remove the psychological barrier between seller and buyer, the more sales you will generate.

How To Remove The Barrier of Entry and Make it Easy For Customers To Buy From You

Imagine the risk customers feel as being a strong *barrier of entry* blocking their purchase. The more you can do to reduce, or elimi-nate the barrier of entry, the greater the number of customers who will buy from you.

You reduce or eliminate the barrier of entry by reversing the risk of the purchase from your customer's shoulders, to your own.

How? By incorporating a **risk reversal philosophy and statement** in your sales message that says to customers, "I un-derstand that you can't be certain this product is **perfect** for you without experiencing it first. Therefore try it or buy it **at my risk,** <u>before</u> you are committed to paying for it. If you are not totally satisfied with it after you get it home, I don't want you to have to pay for it. Simply return it, and I won't charge you a penny.

"But if you agree it has all the benefits I promised it has, pay me at that point and it becomes yours to keep."

That's a **very** powerful sales proposition to put to your cus-tomers. Who in their right mind would refuse?

Afraid Customers Will Take Advantage of You? Here Are The Facts.

Whenever I explain risk reversal at seminars, or to new clients, the same objection is raised: Surely, if you let customers try your

Risk-Reversal:

Removing The Barrier of Entry Between The Seller And The Buyer

1

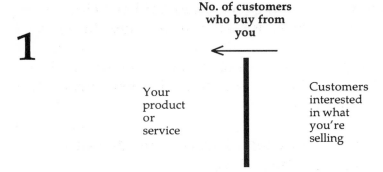

The barrier of entry is high (**No risk reversal applied.**)
Only *limited numbers of customers* will buy from you.

2

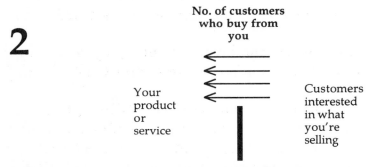

The barrier of entry is *reduced.* (**Some** **risk reversal is applied.**)
More customers will buy from you.

3

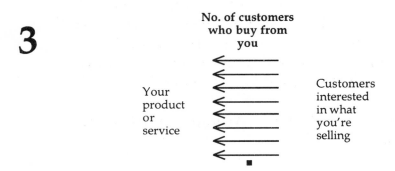

The barrier of entry is eliminated. (**Powerful risk reversal is applied.**)
Maximum number of customers will buy from you.

product before they pay, and return it without owing a penny if they decide to take you up on your guarantee, they'll take advantage of you. You'll lose money hand over fist!

In fact, **the opposite is true.**

The **facts** are these: when you include a powerful risk reversal statement in your sales message, your sales will increase by **up to 300%** while your attrition rate will rarely exceed **5%.**

In sixteen years of marketing I've rarely seen these results differ. What's more, you do not need a 'perfect' product or service to use risk-reversal. If what you are selling will do what you say it will, and it genuinely provides your customers with the value they expect from it, only a small percentage will ask for a refund.

To understand the full sales potential risk-reversal has, you only need do a simple calculation.

In order that you don't accuse me of being overzealous with my figures, let's say your sales increase 50 percent, and your attrition is the highest I've seen — 5 percent.

It's simple to see that 50 percent increase in sales, minus 5 percent returns gives you **42.5 percent** increase in overall sales. (100% original sales plus 50% new sales = 150 x 5% returns = 7.5. 50% increase minus 7.5 = 42.5%.)

Your bottom line **profit** is all that matters. If you can generate substantially more profit by driving up sales through the strategy of risk-reversal *even if it means your attrition rate increases to 5 percent,* who cares?

You've employed a strategy that's left *you* financially enriched; you've increased the perceived and real value of your business in your *customers* eyes by removing the risk they are normally asked to bear.

I was recently asked how I could justify risk-reversal with a high-ticket sale. The question came from an attendee at one of my seminars. He owned a replacement kitchen company.

His question was: *I sell £20,000+ kitchens. Won't people take advantage of me if I give a 100% guarantee of satisfaction?*

My answer is this: Reversing the risk of the purchase from your customer's shoulders to your own is an extremely powerful business-building strategy.

As a *customer* it is unfair for you to receive shoddy workmanship, low quality, low reliability, delayed delivery when you have paid for a product in trust. As a *business* if you know parameters you can work within and the promises you make about your product or service are true, what better way to win customers trust and confidence than to shoulder the burden of risk yourself. After all, the customer is favouring you with his purchase. He shouldn't *have* to take any risk.

Secondly, **the large majority of people are honest.** They don't set out to rip you off. Customers are searching for **value.** That's all.

The more you can say to prospects before the sale: *I promise you value. I promise you expert workmanship. I promise the kitchen I install for you will be constructed from the best materials available. But I want you to see for yourself, and be satisfied what I've said is true, before you commit to paying me. So here's a guarantee that says if you are not 100% satisfied with the work I do, you don't have to pay me.* Customers will line up at your door when you say that.

Remember, the highest attrition rate I've ever seen in sixteen years of marketing is 5 percent. Yet the increase in business you can engineer by reversing the risk of the sale is up to 300 percent. In other words, **you cannot fail to grow your business considerably faster** when you guarantee your product and service.

Let's say you sell 100 kitchens a year, at an average £20,000 each. You make £2,000,000 a year and your gross profit is 15 percent. That's £300,000 profit a year (100 x 20,000 x 15%.)

Let's be conservative and say that by introducing a good risk-reversal statement in all your sales material, you increase your sales by 50 percent. You now sell 150 kitchens at £20,000 x 15% profit — £450,000 profit.

Now let's assume the worst. 5 percent of your customers decide they do not like the kitchen you installed, and ask for their money back. Will you lose out? Or will you make higher profits anyway?

Here's the calculation: 5 percent of 150 kitchens = 7.5, let's say 8. Eight kitchens cost you, say 40% of the selling price in materials = £8,000 each x 8 = £64,000. The labour cost of removing the kitchen is, say £200 per kitchen x 8 = £1,600. So your total attrition cost is £64,000 + £1,600 = £65,600.

Therefore, even though 5 percent took you up on you guarantee **you increased your profit by £84,400** (£150,000 extra profit minus £65,600 attrition.)

That is **28% increase in profits** simply by adding a risk-reversal statement to your sales process (£300,000 + £84,400.)

Do you see how powerful risk-reversal is? What if your attrition rate doesn't reach 5 percent? Most of my clients experience between 0.5 and 2 percent. If your attrition were 1.5 percent — which is probably more likely unless your kitchens are poor value and your workmanship shoddy — with 50 percent increase in sales, look how much your profit increases now:

1.5 percent of 150 kitchens = 2.25, let's call it 3. Three kitchens at 40% cost = £24,000 plus removal labour costs of £200 x 3 kitchens = £600. Total cost £24,600.

Your additional profit has now soared to **£125,400** (£150,000 extra profit minus £24,600 attrition costs.) You've achieved a considerable **41.8 percent increase in profits** (£300,000 + £125,400.)

What's more, because it costs almost nothing to include a risk-reversal statement in your marketing, you make larger profits on every sale.

This is what can happen to your earning power with 50 percent sales increase. But I've seen sales increase up to 300 percent when effective risk-reversal was added to the sales message. You can work out what your profits would be if your sales increased by 150 percent, 200 percent, 250 percent. It's phenomenal.

Change Your Paradigm And Customers Will Beat a Path To Your Door

Why does risk reversal work powerfully? Because it transfers *control* from you the seller, to your customer, the buyer. Customers feel confident buying when they are in control.

For decades, customers have learnt to be wary of sellers. Salespeople have been pushy, tricky, and dishonest. Too many products promise the world but only deliver a trifle. TV consumer-support programmes attract high viewing figures. Consumer magazines like *Which?* in England are amongst top selling publications. All because the customer is desperate to know if he is being deceived by overzealous, or even dishonest sales claims.

But if you know the secrets of direct-response marketing you never have to be overzealous or dishonest to sell high volumes . The opposite is true. The more *customer-oriented* you become, the more your sales will increase.

Change your paradigm from *how much can I sell?* to *how much can I give?* **Add value** to make more money.

The Fastest Way To Sell 1,000,000 Products is to Add *More Value*

How many times have you bought a product or paid for a service and been *amazed* at the value you received? It's rare, isn't it? When it did happen what was your response? If you are like most customers you will have been *impressed, grateful, enthusiastic, motivated to tell other people about it,* and left wanting to *buy more from that organisation.*

That is the stuff of unquantifiable success! I put it to you that if you determine to offer the very best value you can at a profit, you'll sell in greater volumes than you ever will by offering *minimum* value.

One of the most prevailing ways to add tremendous value is to hand control of the sale to your customer by reversing the risk.

Giving control to your customer doesn't put you in a precarious situation. To the contrary. Customers appreciate your openness, honesty and confidence in your product. They realise you aren't just trying to 'take their money'. They see you as a business they can *trust.*

When you reverse the risk of the sale you remove the barrier of entry and customers rush in.

Three Types of Risk Reversal You Can Use

Many business owners are afraid to immediately use the most

powerful form of risk reversal, the *better than risk-free proposal*. They feel safer starting with a lessor guarantee. My advice is this: if you are not using *any* form of risk reversal you are not maximising your sales. But don't rush straight into the better-than-risk-free statement unless you are comfortable using it. Start with the first type and then progress with more powerful types as you see your sales increase.

You can also test different risk-reversal statements at the same time and track the response. Do a split-run test with Type 1 and Type 2, or Type 2 and Type 3, and track the response you receive from each one. You'll soon have the evidence you need to determine which of them is attracting the highest sales. (See Chapter 18: Test And Market The Clear Winner.)

Type 1: The Minimal Risk-Reversal

There is nothing more frustrating than buying a product, getting it home or to the office, and discovering it doesn't work as it should. To my amazement I find many businesses still insist you have to return a faulty product they sold you to the manufacturer for repair. In other words *tough luck* — you bought it from us but we will not accept any responsibility if it doesn't work. If you want an effective way to keep people away from your business, this works well!

It happened to me last month. I needed an additional phone in my office, so I bought a recognised brand from a well known chain of telephone shops. When I made my first call the digit tones didn't sound on half of the numbers. I called the shop, explained the problem and asked if I could replace it. "I'm sorry Sir," the assistant said, "but you'll have to send it back to the manufacturer for repair."

What do you mean I've got to send it to the manufacturer! I just bought it from you one hour ago!

This business, like many others, has no clue of the *psychology* of a sale. The result? I feel cheated and angry. I will *never* buy another product from that shop. In the event, I was told the repair would take 6 weeks so I haven't bothered. But I'm left with an unsatisfactory product.

The smartest policy you can adopt if your product fails in some way is to offer an immediate replacement, or full refund. A happy customer means more sales and more profits in future.

You can attract greater numbers of immediate customers by **stating** your replace-or-refund guarantee boldly in your sales message, rather than just **doing** it if a customer complains.

The key is: **make it a part of your selling message.** Don't hide it in small print. Shout about it boldly in your adverts, sales letters, brochures, flyers, and other marketing.

Here's how to word a typical minimal risk-reversal. Let's say you are a TV store, selling direct to the public.

30-DAY, 100% GUARANTEE

"If, in any way, your new TV has any fault, or develops any defect after you get it home; if it is not in the perfect working condition it was when you saw it in the showroom, simply return it within 30-days and we will replace it on the spot."

"Obviously, in offering you this no-quibble replacement guarantee we are confident that every TV we sell is a quality, reliable, and *tested* model. If we didn't *insist* on selling only the best quality TV's from each manufacturer, we wouldn't dare offer you a 30-day guarantee."

Do you see what this does? You gain competitive advantage because you're telling customers **before the sale** that they are protected if their purchase is in any way faulty. *You have given them a measure of control.*

Your marketing becomes significantly more persuasive than competitors who do not offer this guarantee, or who would replace the TV if asked, *but don't say so up front.*

By even slightly reversing the risk of the sale you have lowered the barrier of entry and more customers will buy from you.

Type 2: The Total Risk Reversal

Here's an example of how to word a total risk-reversal. Using this type you remove *all* the risk the customer feels:

30-DAY, 100% SATISFACTION GUARANTEE

If, *for any reason whatsoever,* you are not completely satisfied with the TV you have bought—the clarity of the picture, fine colour reproduction, and the 'concert hall'

5-speaker surround-sound system... even if you decide after you get it home that you would prefer a different size screen, or a different 'looking' TV—simply return it in new condition within 30 days and we will exchange it, or help you choose a different model, or give you a full refund on the spot, no questions.

With this risk-reversal you're saying to your customer: I don't care what your reason is. If you're not satisfied *for any reason whatsoever* you can return your purchase. I want you to walk away completely delighted no matter what it takes. I value your custom *that much*.

Now you are gaining *considerable* competitive advantage. Which customer, looking for a new TV, wouldn't be compelled by a sales message like this? Why buy a TV from any other store when you can buy from a store that removes the risk of the purchase?

By giving total control to the customer you have lowered the barrier of entry significantly and many more customers will buy from you because they have nothing to lose.

Type 3: The Better-Than-Risk-Free Risk-Reversal

Here is my favourite—the ultimate risk-reversal. You make the purchase entirely risk-free, then offer customers a **free gift** simply for **trying** your product or service.

Crazy? Not when you realise that **volumes more** customers will buy from you. As long as your product does what you promise it will, at least 95 percent will want to keep their purchase.

Here's an example:

100% SATISFACTION GUARANTEE—PLUS VALUABLE FREE GIFT, YOURS TO KEEP

When you buy the ABC TV we'll give you 30 high-resolution blank video tapes worth £107.99, free. Not only that, if *for any reason whatsoever* you are not completely satisfied with the TV you have bought—the clarity of the picture, fine colour reproduction, and the 'concert hall' 5-speaker surround-sound system... even if you decide after you get it home that you would prefer a different size screen, or a different 'looking' TV—simply return it in new condition within 30 days and we will exchange it, or help you choose a different model, or give you a full refund on the spot, no questions. What's more if you do decide to return it and refund on the spot, no questions. What's more if you do decide to return it and receive a refund, you can keep the 30 tapes as a gift for your time.

Use Risk-Reversal No Matter What

Business owners with high-ticket items cry out at my seminars: *That's fine on low price items but it just wouldn't work with cars, or new kitchens, or expensive furniture.*

Entrepreneurs with expendable products like books, food, clothes, etc. say: *That's fine with non-expendable items like a TV or a microwave but I couldn't possibly offer risk-reversal with books. If people return a book I can't resell it!*

Shrewd-thinking proprietors selling duplicatable products like CD's, and audio and video tapes say: *Surely if I allow customers to return a CD they'll rip me off. They'll record the CD and then return it. I'll lose money!*

Service businesses say *they* can't use risk-reversal because they cannot recoup the cost of the service they have provided.

The fact is this: I have seen risk-reversal pull in greater numbers of customers, generate higher sales, and multiply profits faster in practically every type of business you can name, including every type I just mentioned.

You can, and should, use some form of risk-reversal *no matter what you sell.*

CHAPTER 10

Risk-Reversal PART 2
Getting it to Work For You

The owner of the hairdressing and beauty salon I mentioned earlier was worried about offering a risk-free risk-reversal. But after I explained that the **maximum** attrition she would receive was 5 percent, against up to 300 percent increase in sales, she agreed to test it.

We made an introductory beauty therapy offer and tested it to five hundred people in her town. 116 people responded—a 23 percent response. In no way would this number have responded had we not reversed the risk of the sale.

Here's the risk-reversal I wrote in the offer:

"I want you to be completely satisfied with your treatment. So if, for any reason at all, you don't agree it's the most relaxing, invigorating, stimulating and renewing therapy you can experience, if you are disappointed in any way with the tremendous results you will feel with this treatment, **then I don't want you to pay for it.** So, at the end of your treatment, if you are not totally happy with what we have given you, just say so and we won't charge you even the considerably reduced cost of just £24."

How a Curtain Cleaning Company Beat all Sales Records

A curtain cleaning company was beginning to lose sales to three new competitors who were charging less.

I suggested they write to all their existing customers and

include a good risk-reversal; something they had never done.

Despite the new and lower priced competition, their sales beat every other offer they had ever made *even before the competitors arrived on the scene.*

Here's the wording I used:

YOUR COMPLETE SATISFACTION IS GUARANTEED OR WE'LL RE-CLEAN YOUR CURTAINS FREE

Our cleaning service is amongst the most meticulous and personal — and competitively priced — in the country. When you have your curtains cleaned by us I know you will be delighted with the results for a long time after we've re-hung them for you.

Nevertheless, I want to give you this complete satisfaction guarantee. If, *for any reason whatsoever,* you are not absolutely delighted with your freshly cleaned and pressed curtains when we come an re-hang them, *simply tell us and we'll re-clean them completely free of charge.*

Another Strategy Used To Sell The Blind Manufacturers Overstock

After trying numerous ways to sell 15,000 metres of dead inventory over four months, this blind maker asked me to help. I suggested he write to his existing customers, plus neighbouring businesses. One week after he sent the letter every last blind was sold.

This is the risk-reversal statement I wrote into the letter:

"I want you to be completely satisfied with the blinds you buy from me. Although *I* know my workshop makes the very highest quality blinds (we've been making quality blinds for over 16 years now), I want to give you a **30-day, 100% money-back guarantee** with every blind you buy.

"So if, *for any reason whatsoever,* you are not 100% satisfied with the blind you buy when you get it home — if it doesn't look as beautiful as you thought it would, if it doesn't open and close as smoothly and reliably as I said it would, or if the colour isn't as perfect as I described, or <u>any</u> other reason at all — I want you to phone and tell me within 30 days, and I will either replace it for you, or give you a full, 100% refund on the spot, no questions asked.

"Can I be any fairer than that?"

This London Fashion Wholesaler Earned £2.4 Million

It took me three days to persuade a London fashion wholesaler that by adding a powerful risk-reversal statement to his sales proposal, he'd increase his response.

When he finally agreed to let me test it, and the letters were sent to prospective retail customers, he received responses worth £2.4 million of new business.

This is the risk-reversal statement I persuaded him to use:

"I want you to become a stockist **entirely at my risk.** Buy your first amount of stock — on 30-days credit if it helps you. Display it effectively in your shop. Get your local paper to give you free publicity, as I'll show you how. *Then see the reaction of your existing — and new — customers <u>for yourself</u> for the next 30 days.*

"If, after trying the labels for 30 days, you do not agree they will sell as fast in your shop as they are in others — *and keep selling fast* — and that they'll make you £1,000's of extra sales, **simply return the stock that you haven't yet sold and I'll give you a full refund on those garments** and find a different stockist in your area.

"I can't be any fairer than that."

Seven Secrets For Writing a Powerful Risk-Reversal

1. Explain your risk-reversal *in detail*

Don't just say: *If you are not happy with the TV you can return it for an exchange, or a refund.* (Although this would attract more sales than giving no statement.)

Go into detail. Make your product come *alive* in your guarantee. Help your customer to 'see' himself or herself *using* your product, or *experiencing* your service.

2.   Reflect your risk-reversal in your sales message

Risk-reversal shouldn't be an afterthought. You should make it an integral part of your sales message. The more your sales message reflects the idea that your customer *takes no risk by buying your product* the more your sales will increase.

3.   Pack your risk-reversal with positive sales benefits

Many people make the mistake of wording their risk-reversal *negatively.* But to attract the greatest number of sales word it *positively*, with restated sales benefits.

Rather than: *If you don't like the picture quality, sound reproduction, or style of the set... etc.,* reinforce the selling benefits like this: *If you don't think the picture quality is the sharpest, real-life colour reproduction, and the surround-sound quality provides true 'concert hall' effect right in your home, and the integrated styling of the set complements your room.... etc.*

4.   Make your guarantee period as long as you can

Generally, the longer the guarantee period the higher your sales will be.

Customers feel you are attempting to 'trick' them into buying your product if your guarantee period is short. If you say: *take this TV home and try it for 48 hours, and return it if you're not absolutely happy with it,* your customers will probably feel rushed into having to make a quick decision. So *fewer* will take you up on your offer. Seven days would be more powerful. Thirty days more powerful still. Ninety days or longer *very* powerful.

5.   For mail order items, make your guarantee *at least* 14 days

You have to build even more trust when you are selling through the mail. Your customers want to feel you are allowing them enough mailing time to return your product within the specified guarantee period.

The very minimum you should allow is 14 days. But I like to give **long** periods of 90, 120, or 365 days with most products. Why? Because sales increase dramatically!

If you cannot resell a returned product, why worry? The extra sales you've achieved because of your risk-reversal — up to three hundred percent increase in sales — far outstrips any losses you'll incur through returns.

At the end of the day you're only interested in **profits.** If you can bank 50%, 100%, 500%, 1,000% or more extra profits by including a powerful risk-reversal statement in your sales message, you're growing your business faster.

I've seen results of this magnitude often. When you can increase your sales by up to three hundred percent from the same marketing pieces *without incurring extra marketing costs* your profits grow exponentially.

6.   Make it *easy* for customers to return your product

If you make it sound difficult to return your product less prospects will respond. Make it *easy.* Say, "Simply return it within 90 days, and we'll replace it for you on the spot, or give you a full, 100% refund immediately."

Or, "If there is *anything* you are not happy with when we deliver the car, just tell us and we'll have it corrected free, or give you a full refund on the spot."

Or, "If there is any aspect of the computer you're not entirely happy with, simply phone us and we'll send an engineer out to correct it, or give you a 100%, no-quibble refund on the spot."

7.   Make it *easy* for customers to ask for a refund when you're providing a service

Most people feel uncomfortable asking for a refund face-to-face. So put even more importance on the ease in which a customer can take up your guarantee. Make people feel that you genuinely do not want to take their money unless they are completely and utterly satisfied with the service you've provided.

Say, "If you are not 100% delighted with your freshly dry-cleaned curtains, simply say so when we re-hang them for you and we'll re-clean them completely free of charge."

Or, "At the end of your beauty treatment, if you are not totally happy with what we've given you, just say so and we won't charge you a penny. I don't want you to pay unless your 100% pleased."

Dive Straight In!

Our whole culture has brought us up to believe we *win* when we get a sale. But we've been brought up wrong. We only truly win when we help our customers win too.

Risk-reversal helps your customers win too. When you're as bold as to say, *I don't just want to take your money, I want to be paid only by giving you great value,* customers will recognise your intention and line up at your door.

For most business owners risk-reversal is a scary strategy. Don't be frightened of it. Dive straight in! You'll quickly see a surge of new customers come through the 'barrier', be satisfied, recommend you to their family, friends, colleagues.

You'll see your sales soar and your profits multiply exponentially. **Risk-reversal is now *your* secret weapon as well as mine.**

Next—find out why it's vital that you: **Market To Your Intended Customers Only...**

CHAPTER 11

Market To Your Intended Customers Only

It is all too easy to dissipate your marketing. I see hundreds of costly adverts, brochures, blow-ins, inserts, posters, and others, that could produce multiples more response at no extra cost if only they targeted, and appealed to the most likely type of customers the product or service would sell to.

Become a Customer and You'll See Why

To understand this you have to become a customer. Take a minute to step inside the mind of a customer who wants to buy, say, a new Hi-Fi system. Isn't it true that when you've set your heart on buying something, you become *passionate* about it. You'd be excited about going off to buy a new Hi-Fi.

You wake up early Saturday morning thinking about getting it. You get the newspapers and Hi-Fi magazines. You scour the pages for reviews, prices, best buys, comparisons between different systems, even style. (Many people choose styling over functionality.)

You become *focused* on Hi-Fi's, don't you?

Now, do you think anyone else in your town is planning to buy a Hi-Fi the same day you do? Of course! Thousands of Hi-Fi's are sold everyday throughout the country. Tens or maybe hundreds will be sold *in your town* the same day you buy yours. Do you think all those customers might also be focused on Hi-Fi's that day? You bet. It's human nature.

As you search the Hi-Fi ads, are you more attracted to the store with 230 units in stock for you to choose from—everything from compact midi systems to mega separates, competitive prices, and sales assistants who know what they're talking about?

Or are you drawn to stores that stock some Hi-Fi's, some washing machines, some PC's, some vacuum cleaners, and some microwaves?

Which one?

When you want a Hi-Fi, you don't care very much about washing machines, PC's, vacuum cleaners or microwaves. You only care about Hi-Fi's. You're *focused* on Hi-Fi's!

The same applies with almost everything people buy. The exceptions are low-priced, everyday products. Otherwise, you are going to be *interested, passionate,* and *focused,* on what you are buying.

Keep Your Marketing *Focused* To Capture The Maximum Number Of Customers—And Sales

How do you increase your sales by knowing that customers are focused when they buy?

Focus your sales message directly at them, and no one else.

If you ran a specialist Hi-Fi store your task would be simpler; you put out marketing about Hi-Fi's only.

But let's say you own an electrical store that sells Hi-Fi's, washing machines, PC's, vacuum cleaners and microwaves.

Would you achieve the highest sales by running ads featuring all your products like most multi-product stores do? (Look in any newspaper.)

Or would you do better to focus your sales message to one category of buyer at a time?

The answer lies with you, the Hi-Fi buyer. You are more likely to be interested in the **specialist store** that stocks a wide selection of Hi-Fi's at competitive prices because you would expect to see a wider choice, and to receive more expertise. The store that sells Hi-Fi's plus washing machines, plus PC's, plus vacuum cleaners, plus microwaves, probably will not have the same choice or expertise.

The two respected marketing strategists Al Ries and Jack Trout say in their book *The 22 Immutable Laws of Marketing**, "The essence of marketing is **narrow focus.** You become stronger when you reduce the scope of your operations. You can't stand for something if you chase after everything."

When you narrow your focus you start making more money. Lots more money.

You will attract multiples more Hi-Fi buyers to your store by featuring *only* Hi-Fi's in your advert and other sales messages.

Likewise, feature *only* washing machines when you want to attract most washing machine buyers, *only* PC's when you want to attract most PC buyers, *only* vacuum cleaners when you want to attract most vacuum cleaner buyers... you get the idea.

The More You Focus The More You Sell

Many clients I first explain this to say, "That's all very well, but if I only promote one of my products I'll lose out on all the customers who want to buy my other stuff."

Surely that's true, right? Wrong.

It's true you won't attract any other category of buyer from your focused Hi-Fi ad. **But you will attract many more Hi-Fi buyers because you are talking directly, and only, to them.**

In marketing, less is more and more is less.

Less diversity = More sales

More diversity = Less sales

In people's minds they buy **one** thing at a time. So speak to your customer as if what you are selling is all they are buying.

*The 22 Immutable Laws of Marketing, by Al Ries & Jack Trout, 1993, Harper Business

Focus your sales message on your intended customer, and no one else.

Your sales appeal should shout loudly at every person interested in Hi-Fi:

"If you're buying a new Hi-Fi this week, you <u>must</u> read this message..."

That kind of headline is going to grab the attention of almost everyone buying a Hi-Fi. *By being specific you attract umpteen more prospective buyers.*

Recognise your customer as an individual, interested, focused buyer of one product or service at a time. The more you focus and specialise your sales message, the more you will sell and the greater profit you will make.

Now discover: **How To Target Your Most Ready-to-Buy Customers...**

CHAPTER 12

How To Target Your Most Ready-to-Buy Customers

If you were trying to target the source of a fire so that you could quickly control the flames and then extinguish them, you would adjust your fire hose to shoot a powerful, focused jet of water directly at the source.

You would never think to use a wide, dissipated spray to reach the source of the fire. If you did, you would waste a large amount of the water you were spraying, take longer to extinguish the fire, and waste much of your effort.

A prospective customer interested in your offer is like the source of a fire. If your marketing message is not targeted directly at him or her, you waste a large portion of your funds, time, and effort.

Obviously, you want to *optimize* your funds and effort, not waste them. Each marketing move you make should generate greater profits.

Hone your sales messages, particularly your **headlines and opening statements** to instantly and specifically capture the interest of customers who are *ready* to buy what you are selling.

Here's how.

If you were selling a new carpet cleaning liquid that more effectively removed stubborn stains, and you ran ads in national magazines, radio, and on T.V., you will dissipate your message if you use 'clever' headlines or opening statements like:

"A Solution for Every Household"

or,

"A Solution Your Carpet Will Love"

or,

"With Kids Around, You Could Do With This Solution"

Without exception abstract and circuitous sales messages like these do not pull anywhere near the maximum response you can achieve when you use a targeted approach.

How To Target Your Sales Messages With Pinpoint Accuracy

How do you target more accurately? Simply speak *plainly* and *directly* to the needs of the person your product or service will benefit.

Put out sales messages that *qualify* your reader, listener, or viewer. For example, you could say:

"If your carpet has a stubborn wine, coffee, or mud stain, new instant-acting *Stain Dissolver* will wipe it away in just seconds"

You would then go on to explain the benefits and *reasons-why* your cleaning liquid can dissolve stains in seconds. (See Chapter 8)

If you were selling men's fashion, you'd be unwise to run ads that said:

"For The Man About Town"

or,

"For The Man Who Wants To Impress"

Headlines like this do not mean anything. They are just cutesy. They're trying to be clever. But cutesy and clever do not appeal to anywhere near the number of prospects who would respond to a more credible approach.

Instead, you should run ads that are factual, targeted, and informative:

"Looking for a £65 shirt for just £29? We've got 250 in stock this Saturday"

or,

"If you're looking for a smart 2-piece, pure wool suit, we have 200 in stock right now, at prices you won't beat"

If you were a photographer, and you were available for weddings, parties, family portraits, and pet portraits, instead of saying something like:

"Photography for weddings, parties, family portraits, pet portraits. Phone 0171 123 1234"

Be more specific. Speak to one prospective customer at a time. Target your message to the individual who is looking for a specific type of photography:

"Would you like the type of wedding photographs that are loved and admired forever? I have photographed over 500 weddings. Every Bride and Groom has said they are the most beautiful photos they could have asked for. If you phone 0800 123 1234 I'll send you a free

colour brochure that'll show you — scene by scene through a real wedding — how beautiful *your* wedding photos can be too. I think you'll also be interested in the price."

Do you see how much more *compelling* this message is? Do you see how it will seek out the prospects looking for this type of photography and impact them more *powerfully?*

Apply the same techniques for your product or service. Explain it fully, in plain, straightforward, 'street-talk'. Ninety-five percent of customers all over the world are unassuming, street-talking folk. When you communicate with them through your marketing in the same way you would *talk* to them in the pub, you will appeal to them on their own level, and they'll respond in bigger numbers.

5 Golden Rules For Effective Customer Targeting

1.   Aim your headlines and opening phrases directly at the *individual* person you are trying to sell to.

2.   Never be cutesy, clever, humorous, or circuitous. It's a waste of your time and marketing money.

3.   Always explain what real *benefit, result, advantage* your product or service will give your customer.

     Remember people only want to know **what's in it for me?**

4.   Use *long, interesting, pertinent* copy.

     Use as many headline words (up to seventeen) and as much body copy as you need to fully explain your offer. Remember, your sales message cannot be too *long*. Only too *boring*.

5.   Get into the mind of the customer when targeting your sales message. "What's in it for me?"

What would he or she most *want* from your product or service. Once you have identified that, you can target accurately.

Turn quickly now to Part 3 and discover: **How To Write Sales Letters, Adverts, Flyers, Inserts & Brochures That SELL...**

PART 3

How to Write Sales Letters, Adverts, Flyers, Inserts, Brochures That SELL

CHAPTER 13

The Key To Writing
Sales Letters That SELL

Millions of pounds of marketing tests which track the type and style of sales message that people respond to in greatest quantity have proven conclusively:

Customers respond to *letters* more than
any other piece of paper

I regularly see businesses with a good product or service send out literature *without an accompanying letter*. Or a letter so weak it may as well not have been sent.

These businesses could multiply their results by doing nothing more than *writing a good sales letter* to accompany their literature.

A good letter will out-pull a brochure, flyer, blow-in, post-card—even a sample video, or cassette—by up to 10:1. It's **that** effective.

Why? Because a letter is the oldest form of communicating one to one.

- It's **traditional;** we feel **comfortable** receiving a friendly letter.
- It's **personal;** it has been written for **you.**
- It's **flattering:** someone has taken the time and trouble to sit down and share useful information, news, education, and opportunity **with you.**

Companies spend £1,000's equipping their sales team with glossy sales literature stuffed with facts, figures, charts, graphs, photographs, samples; they send sales teams on expensive training courses; give them nice cars, and expense accounts.

Quite rightly, each sales person should be fully able to provide the full sales story to every prospective customer. He or she should be in a position to show a prospect all the benefits, advantages and reasons-why what they are selling will bring value to the customer's life in one way or another, or in a number of ways.

All this effort, time and expense is assigned to maximising field sales. But often when an interested customer calls for details about that business's product or service, all that is sent is a colour brochure, a photocopied price list, a photocopied list of nearest stockists, with either **no** letter, or a short, to the point, one-page letter that stands *little chance if any* of compelling a prospect to buy.

Without realising their mistake, businesses sending out literature like this are receiving only a *fraction* of the sales they could be garnering **if they simply sent an interesting sales letter too.**

This Company's Mistake is Costing Them £100,000's in Lost Sales

As if they knew I was writing this chapter, one company provided me with a perfect example to show you! But they are only one of *thousands* of businesses making the same mistake.

As the cold weather was setting in this winter I came across a full page colour ad in one of the Sunday supplements advertising an attractive range of freestanding electric radiators. We live in a 16th Century home which on the coldest of days leaves one or two rooms in need of a little extra heating! So the ad caught my eye.

The ad didn't explain much about the range but asked readers to call for more details. This I did and a few days later the details arrived.

The envelope contained the following: a one-page, full colour A4 leaflet, a photocopied list of leading stockists, and a photocopied letter. Take a look at their letter, reproduced on the next

116

page. (I have changed a few details to protect the company but otherwise the letter is exactly as received.)

The 7 Cardinal Mistakes This Letter Makes and How To Avoid Them in *Your* Letters

Mistake #1:

It is not *personal*. The salutation does not say *Dear Mr Gorman* even though I gave the company my name. Instead they've used a general salutation *Dear Consumer*.

If you have a prospect's name, use it!

Why? Have you ever turned your head when you heard your name being called in a busy street? Yes! We all have! But why on earth did you think the person was shouting for **you?** Because we all love our own names. Our name is our personal identity. Whenever we hear it announced or see it on paper **we pay attention.** Always address people by their proper name.

If they have a title (Doctor, Sir etc.), use it. In most cases, avoid being familiar; on the whole people don't appreciate it. If a person gives you their name as *John Smith*, your salutation should usually be *Dear Mr Smith*, not *Dear John*—unless and until they **ask** to be called by their first name, or you **are sure** they will appreciate it.

Mistake #2:

It has no compelling *headline* or *opening sentence*. Why should I be interested in spending my money on **this** radiator? Why is it better (produces more heat per unit of energy, heats a room faster, cheaper to run, lighter in weight, etc.) than any other radiator on the market?

Mistake #3:

It doesn't explain the benefits or differences between each heater in their range. How do I know which one will suit me best? Which size is most suitable for which size of room? Have they got one that is more efficient than the others? Their USP is: **The Only Heater Worth Buying.** Why is this? What advantages

```
+-----------------+
|    COMPANY      |
|    LOGO         |
+-----------------+
```

Date as Postmarked

Dear Consumer

Thank you for your recent enquiry about the new ABC Heater from XYZ Electric.

We have enclosed product literature on this and our other heating products.

The ABC Heater is available from all well known High Street electrical stores and independant retailers.

Retail prices range from £49.99 for the 110X to £103.99 for the 222X. Please see your nearest stockist for details.

However, should you have any difficulty in locating you local stockist or have any further queries, please contact us at our Customer Services department on (Telephone number).

Yours faithfully

Customer Services.

A typical letter sent in reply to a customer's request for more information - it has little chance of compelling customers to buy has it got over others? As a potential customer I want and need this information to help me make a wise buying decision.

Mistake #4

It looks tatty. It is a photocopied piece of paper (not even a good photocopy) instead of a quality printed letter. What image does this conjure up about the company? It doesn't care? It is shoddy? It does not *value* me enough as a prospective customer to provide me with quality literature?

Mistake #5

It makes me feel one of the crowd, not individual. Did you also notice on the top left: Date as Postmarked? It should have a date, as if it were written for me individually on the date I inquired.

Mistake #6

There is no signature. They have sent me a letter from their anonymous 'customer services' department. I don't want customer services! I want the **Sales Director** or the **Chairman** to take the trouble and interest to write to me and lead me through his range of heating appliances. **Always, always** sign your letters *personally.*

(By the way, I see many sales letters signed with a 'PP'. If you receive a letter like this, what does it tell you? It tells you the 'important' person in the company hasn't got time to sign it him or herself. So they've had their secretary sign it. It is an insult to customers. **Never, never** use a 'PP' signature on any letter.)

Mistake #7

There is no P.S. This letter is missing a powerful selling opportunity by not including a value-based P.S. (See Chapter 14.)

The overall impression this letter gives is *they don't care enough about their product or their prospective customers to send a personalised, detailed, neat letter.* In no way does this encourage me to buy their product.

Now, I am sure this company *does* care. And I happen to

know they *do* have a good product. But they are missing out on the significant additional sales they could garner *for no extra cost* because their letter is ineffective.

A Sales Letter is Simply Salesmanship in Print

The secret of writing a powerful, interesting letter that will multiply your sales is realising that:

A sales letter is simply Salesmanship-in-Print

You would never dream of sending your salespeople out to a prospect only to have them dump your brochure, a list of prices, and a couple of ordering details on the desk, would you? Your prospect wants — and needs — much more detail and information about your offer in order to make a wise buying decision.

For the same reason, you should never send a sales letter that does not fully explain all the benefits and advantages your product or service offers.

Think of a sales letter as nothing less than **your salesperson in an envelope.**

I say to business owners at seminars: record on cassette tape the process your best salesperson goes through in front of a prospect. Then transcribe it almost word for word and there you have a great sales letter.

10 Rules For Writing Winning Sales Letters

Rule #1
Open with a powerful, compelling, interesting, and persuasive **headline** or **opening statement** (See Chapter 5: The Million Pound Sales Secret.)

Rule #2
Tell the full story. Just as your sales *person* would spend time with your prospective customer, so your sales *letter* should explain the full benefits, advantages and reasons-why of your product or service. It should lead your reader by the hand through

the benefits and advantages he or she will gain by buying your product.

Rule #3

Use everyday language. Write as you would **talk.** Make your style **conversational** rather than formal.

95 percent of customers are modest, everyday, roll-your-sleeves-up people. If you write in a highfaluting, forced style, it doesn't ring true with people and they discard your message.

Again, it is invaluable to record on tape the way you or your best salesperson talk to customers. Transcribe it almost word for word, including all the abbreviations. It will read more fluently.

Rule #4

Realise that every customer out there experiences the same everyday problems you and I experience. They are human beings experiencing the niggles of life like everyone else. They sometimes get headaches. They sometimes worry about money. They sometimes get into arguments. They get frustrated, annoyed, mad.

When you write, try to understand what your reader might be feeling. Recognise their problems and frustrations, and sympathise with them. Be on their side.

The more your offer *helps people solve a problem or fulfil a desire or need* the greater number of sales you'll make.

Rule #5

Include a compelling Call-To-Action. Why should your prospect order now? Also, make ordering easy. Lead your reader through the ordering or buying process so that he or she knows exactly how to buy your product or service (See Chapter 6.)

Rule #6

Include a P.S. Restate your main selling benefit, or add a new benefit or bonus (See Chapter 14.)

Rule #7

Sign your letter in **process blue ink** (Cyan), and no other colour. Thousands of tests have shown people respond more to a process blue signature. Don't make the mistake of thinking that your signature, or the **colour ink** you sign with, will not affect your sales results. It will, and does, by extraordinary amounts. Always sign in a legible, confident manner. Big and wild, or tiny and scraggy don't work to exude the balanced, believable image you want to portray.

Rule #8

Make your letter *look* like a letter. Don't fancy it up with artwork, cartoons, and graphics. These 'clever' additions turn out to be **not** so clever, because **response drops** the fancier a letter looks. Design your letter to look neat, and well laid-out. But keep it looking like a *letter.*

Rule #9

Always use **Courier** or **Times Roman** letter font. Why? Because millions of pounds of tests have shown conclusively that **people respond more to these two fonts** than any other. Change them at your peril.

Rule #10

Use the 7-Step Formula in Chapter 6 to construct your letter (How To Keep Your Customers Riveted To Your Sales Message.) It's a sales-proven process of guiding your prospect from initial interest, through to buying.

7 Big-Selling Letters

Letter #1

Remember the fashion wholesaler I mentioned earlier? He imported chic club and party wear from Paris to sell to retail boutiques throughout the UK. Within twelve weeks of applying the strategies in this book, his business grew from a fledgling £500,000 to a sales value of £2,400,000. All with a peppercorn marketing budget of £2,800.

What was the secret? Like most business owners, this entrepreneur's approach to sales did not differentiate him from his competitors. He telemarketed boutiques, announced his range of fashion, and asked if he could send further details. Six in ten said *yes*.

But his information pack was ineffective — a business-type letter (like the one on page 118), and some colour pictures of his range.

He then followed up with a second call to try to get an order. His system was time consuming and failed to produce much result. Yet his range of clothing was *exciting*.

I suggested two strategies that would grow his business substantially. First, we shifted his business paradigm from *how much can I sell to boutiques?* to, *how much can I help boutiques sell larger quantities of my range?*

The whole concept of his business changed from **getting as much as possible** to, **adding as much *value* as possible.**

Second, I suggested we prepare an interesting mailer that would grab boutique owners attention, differentiate him from every other wholesaler, and demonstrate his ability to add value to the boutique owner's business.

The package we sent consisted of: a letter, a Twinings™ tea bag, seven beautifully reproduced double-sided A4 colour pages of his range, an order form, and a reply-paid return envelope.

The key to the mailing was the *letter*. Here it is in full (see pages 124 - 126).

Letter #2

In 1982 I teamed up with a rock and jazz-rock electric guitarist and wrote a seven-part audio tape and workbook home study course. It was the first of its type at the time and attracted a lot of attention.

I marketed it with a two-step system; ads in the national music press told budding guitar players about the course we'd developed and offered them a free pack of information if they returned the coupon.

The information pack consisted of: a letter, an A3 brochure detailing the course, an order form, and a reply paid envelope.

The letter produced a consistent 20 percent response for over 5 years (see pages 128-129.)

continued on page 127...

NAME OF COMPANY
Address, Telephone, Fax

<u>Before</u> You Read About a Nationally Featured, Fast-Selling Fashion Offer I'd Like <u>Your Shop</u> To Participate in... Have a Cup of Tea on Me!

Dear Boutique Owner,

This letter contains an offer that can make you an extra <u>£31,500 sales</u>. That's the average amount of extra sales our participating shops <u>are already making</u>. If you do better than average you can make a lot more.

That's why I've included a fresh tea bag with your letter! Quite honestly, I don't want you to rush through it like the rest of your morning post.

<u>Please take 2 minutes to boil your kettle and have a cup of tea on me</u>. Then you can read my offer while you're sipping!

If your shop sells to young girls and women - from ages 16 to 30 - you can make an average of £31,500 extra sales with a new, yet already booming line of club and party fashion. Some shops are already making a lot more.

I own the exclusive rights to a line of extraordinary club gear that is attracting so much national press and magazine coverage that <u>sales have boomed over 390% - yes **390%** - in the last eleven months</u>.

Shops that started buying small 'test' amounts of stock in October 1994 - £215 to £500 at wholesale - are now experiencing so much demand that they're buying **three to ten times this amount every month to keep up with sales**.

Why is it selling like crazy? To be honest, I don't know for sure. All I know is the three labels - (name of labels) - are a real eye-catcher. The designs are exciting. Girls know they'll look different with this gear on. *And they're buying it as if it won't be available next month.*

Three weeks ago top model (name of model) walked through the door of my wholesale shop in London. She'd seen some of the pictures in *Cosmopolitan* magazine and come straight along. She walked out with £2,800 worth of gear to wear on her latest video and pop tour.

<u>But not before I was able to get her to pose for a few pictures!</u> I've enclosed two of them for you. (Sorry about the poor quality, but I only had an 'instant' camera on me.)

The top London model agency (name of model agency) phoned me after seeing all the press coverage. They want to use all three labels for their models on assignments. *Many of these pictures will be used in the national press and copies will be available for our stockists to use as sales-inspiring window, wall and counter promotions.*

Press, magazine and TV. features are still flooding in. So far, here's a list of the coverage the labels have attracted:

- 1 -

The letter that grew my clients business from £500,000 to £2.4 million
Page 1

- *Girl About Town* magazine, 2nd October
- GMTV Passion for Fashion, 20th October
- HTV, 31st October
- *Joy* magazine, November
- *TV Quick,* November issue
- *The Sun,* 1st November
- *More* magazine, November issue
- *Daily Mirror,* 9th November
- *Shout* magazine, Nov/Dec issue
- *19* magazine, December issue
- BBC 1's *Clothes Show* magazine, December issue
- *Cosmopolitan* magazine, January magazine
- *More* magazine, January issue
- *Looks* magazine, January magazine
- *It's Bliss* magazine, February issue

With this amount of national media attention, is it any wonder shops are selling more of these labels than any other line they stock?

Do you want to become one of my stockists? With exclusive rights to all three labels in your area? If the answer is "yes," I would like to make you a very special offer.

But there is a catch. In fact *four.*

First, the three labels are good quality, fast selling and exclusive. They're attracting a lot of media attention, as you've seen. For this reason, your shop has to be a quality retailer. One which your customers like coming back to time and time again.

Second, your customers must be aged between 16 and 30. Frankly, these labels will not succeed with older customers.

Third, I know from our existing stockists the labels sell fastest when you display a good range. If you just display half-a-dozen garments <u>the labels won't sell well.</u> You won't attract sufficient customers to sell the 10's and 100's of garments you can with a fuller display.

For this reason, I'd ask that you are willing to start with a stock level of between £500 to £1,000 minimum at wholesale. This will give you an exciting enough initial display - enough to get the girls in and word-of-mouth started.

Fourth, *I cannot supply every shop that responds.* Each one of my stockists has an exclusive area. No other shop within an agreed distance can hold the stock. That way, <u>you can sell the labels at full mark-up because your customers won't be able to buy them anywhere else near you.</u>

But it means many of the shops that respond to this letter will have to be turned down. If you are seriously interested in selling these exciting labels, ***<u>please respond today.</u>***

As long as these four 'catches' are not a stumbling block for you - and hopefully they're not - then I'd like to make you an offer that I think will help you make thousands of extra sales this year.

There is going to be a lot more publicity on the labels this year. So I need to quickly take on around one hundred extra shops throughout the U.K. as official stockists. At the moment I am being inundated with calls from girls who've seen all the press articles wanting to know where they can buy the labels locally. <u>I am actually losing hundreds of thousands of pounds of sales because I haven't got stockists in enough areas.</u>

- 2 -

This includes your area.

So my offer is this. If you help me by responding quickly - <u>by the 23rd February at the latest</u> - *and as long as another shop in your area hasn't responded before you* - I'll give you **30-days credit on as much stock as you want to start with** (with the minimum £500 to £1,000 - subject to status.)

I'll give you details of exactly how the existing stockists are displaying the labels in their shops for maximum sales, show you how to get hundreds of pounds of free publicity in your local paper, and help you - on an ongoing basis - to build the label in your area to maximum sales and maximum profits.

I'll provide you with free posters and photo display cards too, that are helping to boost sales dramatically in every one of our stockists.

One more thing. It's important.

I want you to become a stockist **entirely at my risk.**

Buy your first amount of stock - on 30-days credit if it helps you. Display it effectively in your shop. Get your local paper to give you free publicity, as I'll show you. *Then see the reaction of your existing - and new - customers <u>for yourself</u> for the next 30 days.*

If, after trying the three labels for 30 days, you do not agree they will sell as fast in your shop as they are in others - *and keep selling fast* - that they'll make you £1,000's of extra sales, **simply return the stock that you haven't yet sold, and I'll give you a full refund on those garments** and find a different stockist in your area.

I can't be any fairer than that.

On this **NO-RISK, FULL MONEY-BACK** basis, fill out the New Stockists form **enclosed and return it in the reply paid envelope today.**

Or if you prefer, call me today on 0171 000 0000.

Yours sincerely,

(Name of Owner)
(Name of Company)

P.S. It's rare that a fashion label takes off so quickly these days. It's unusual that a label attracts a barrage of prominent national press, magazine and television publicity.

Perhaps it's just pure luck that a national star like (name of famous model) has decided to 'adopt' the range as her official outfits for stage performances and video shoots, with all the accompanying publicity she will attract.

But however rare, unusual or lucky, <u>these labels are hot property.</u> *Don't miss the opportunity of selling this exciting range to the hundreds of club and party goers in your area.*

- 3 -

Letter #3

I wrote this letter for my beauty therapy client. The owner had put a lot of money and effort into opening her salon but was getting a poor response to her ads.

I suggested she stop advertising and make an offer to the employees of all the major companies in her town *with their blessing* (see Chapter 23). We liaised with six large companies and in each case gave a *reason-why* we were offering such a good introductory price to their staff. (The letter I am showing here was to staff of one of the big banks.)

The two page letter (shown on pages 130-131) was given by hand to five hundred employees **with their wages.** It produced a remarkable 22 percent response and filled her appointment diary solid for three months. Cost? Just £103 for printing.

Letters #4 and #5

These two letters attracted enough new business to keep my client busy, and making big profits, for over a year. Then he simply sent them out again. That was ten years ago. Last time I spoke to him he told me he still uses the same letters to this day whenever he wants to boost business.

He owns a highspeed copy shop, and I figured he could get a lot of business from printers who are too busy to deal with copying jobs, but could make extra money if they did.

I proposed in the first letter that they give all their copy jobs to my client, who would in turn give them a share of the profits. We had to assure these printers that we weren't interested in 'stealing' their customers. (See letter on page 132.)

The second letter went out to every business in his catchment area, suggesting they give their bigger copying requirements to my client. They did! (See letter on page 133.)

Letter #6

continued on page 134...

ROCKMASTER PUBLICATIONS

You Can Become a Successful Lead Guitarist Playing at 'Professional' Standard Within Just Weeks!

Dear Bob,

How many times have you thought, "If only I could spend a few precious hours with the best professional Lead Guitarist I know, so that he could actually show me how to play." This would surely be the most enjoyable and effective learning method ever!

We certainly believe it is and so we went out and found a really top rate lead guitarist - Robert Francis - and invited him to come and help us record a complete Course of Electric Lead and Rhythm playing instruction. He did! And what we've ended up with is we believe, 'the most unique Electric Guitar learning programme ever put together.'

A bold statement... true. But just look at how it works.

Just as if he were sitting right next to you, Robert Francis speaks to you on cassette tapes, explaining lead and rhythm techniques and methods and then plays 'live' examples so that you can hear exactly how every lead run and rhythm passage should sound.

Then it's your turn. Switch off the cassette and have a go at reproducing the sound you heard, on your guitar! Flick the cassette back on and find Robert talking to you about what you just played - giving you hints on how to make it sound better, how to improve your playing quickly. And with his hints you find you really do improve fast!

Within minutes you are actually playing exciting lead runs and chord sequences. Within a few hours you are playing them well. Within a few days you are ready to move on to the next section! This method has been tried and tested and proved to be this fast.

"But," you will say, "if I really had my favourite lead guitarist sitting right next to me, he would actually be listening to my playing, telling me how to play everything better, and showing me how he does it." It is here that the Rockmaster Course really justifies the title 'unique'.

PLEASE READ THIS CAREFULLY: You are given the opportunity to actually record rock solos and rhythm tracks and send them on a cassette tape to Robert Francis, who will personally listen to your

Please turn over...

This letter for a home study music course produced a consistant 20% response
Page 1

playing and then <u>speak direct to you</u> on tape, telling you how to improve your techniques and playing ability!! Just the same as if he were sitting right next to you.

This is no 'play with words' - he actually listens to your playing and speaks direct to you.

We are so convinced that, using our method, you will learn electric guitar <u>faster</u> and <u>better</u> than you ever thought possible, we make you this promise:

Using the Rockmaster method you can learn to play to a standard you never dreamed possible. You will be able to turn out 'professional class' sounds and you can become easily good enough to join a professional band for recording and live work. This is our promise. And we also promise that no other method will get you there so fast.

But we don't expect you to go on a promise only. So we guarantee it. In fact, we're willing to give you a whole three weeks to decide whether you like our method:

We GUARANTEE that if for <u>any reason whatsoever</u> you do not agree that our method will do everything we say it will, that it is the best, fastest and most unique method of learning electric guitar, then you can return all the material you have received in 21 days and we will immediately make you a full refund - no questions asked.

Could we offer anything fairer than that?

On the strength of this guarantee we ask you to try our method. We have enclosed an enrolment form and prepaid envelope for you to use.

So don't hesitate - order your Rockmaster course today! Remember you can't lose anything. Our unique, RISK-FREE guarantee is your safeguard.

Yours sincerely,

Paul Gorman

P.S. FREE BONUS: If you order quickly - by 15th October latest - we'll send you a free copy of the book, "How To Set-up a Mini Recording Studio at Home." It shows you how to set up a fully operational 4-track recording studio at low, low cost and how to make yourself sound 'professional' on tape. It's yours to keep even if you decide to ask for a refund.

Important Announcement to all (Company) Staff...

Here's a Special Treat For all Your Hard Work...

Dear (name of company) Staff Member,

How would you like to spend four and a half hours with me and come out feeling totally relaxed yet invigorated, refreshed and feeling on top of the world?

Now you can... with a 'top-to-toe relaxation and invigoration therapy that will make you feel like a completely new person. Best of all - **because you are a staff member at** (company) - I have arranged for you to get an amazing 70% discount for your first visit. (I have a special reason for giving (company) staff this big discount, which I'll tell you about later in this letter.)

The benefits of skilful body massage to increase blood flow and make your muscles more supple, the use of high grade essential oils and plant extracts to invigorate and refresh your skin, and the application of pedicure treatments to revitalise and stimulate your feet and legs, have long been known. **Now you can try it - at a price you won't believe - and feel the amazing benefits yourself.**

Here's the complete therapy package you can have - one for women, one for men.

Women: You'll start by being given a full facial therapy treatment. Using the famous Darphin high grade essential oils and plant extracts, your facial skin will first be deep cleansed and then condition with blends that work by interacting on all three layers of your skin.

You are then treated to a full aromatherapy back, shoulder and scalp massage that will relax you like never before. This is often the favourite part of the process for many people. **It leaves you feeling that good!** The reason it works so effectively is because the massage and use of essential oils work on the deeper levels of your tissue, stimulating your blood and lymph.

There is something particularly relaxing about receiving a peppermint pedicure. When you relax and bath your feet, you tend to feel the benefit throughout the rest of your body too. Have you ever just bathed your feet in a bowl of warm water at the end of a busy day? That's how the peppermint pedicure feels - except ten times more relaxing!

You start off relaxing your feet in a warm, stimulating jacuzzi and then receive a leg and foot massage with peppermint and sweet almond oil to help relieve your tired muscles.

Next - a skin colour consultation. Have you ever had a professional make-up artist advise you which colours best suit your complexion and facial structure? Using 'your' colours and shades makes a tremendous difference to the way you look. We'll show you how to bring out your best features, how to choose particular colours for your skin type and eye colour. We'll explain each stage to you so you can duplicate the effect at home.

Finally, **you are invited to have your hair styled with one of our top stylists.** You can discuss various different styles, have a cut that is completely different from your usual style, or go for what you normally have. One thing though. Our stylists are highly qualified professionals. If you have any problems or challenges with your hair, the stylist will talk you through and show you how to solve your hair problem.

Many problems like flat hair, uncontrollable hair or unevenness can be solved with a quality cut. Let us know if you want to 'change' any particular frustrating aspect of your hair. We'll do our best to solve it for you and show you how to maintain it at home.

Men: You start with a full body aromatherapy massage. Aromatherapy is an ancient healing

Please turn over...

This letter pulled a big 22% response for a beauty salon
Page 1

art that uses essential oils from fruits, flowers, seeds, gums, leaves and resins, firmly massaged over your body. By concentrating at known therapeutic pressure points, you become entirely relaxed and invigorated. A wonderful experience that you'll feel for days afterwards.

We then give you a full facial therapy to deep cleanse your skin of dead cells and ingrained debris that is not removed by normal soap washing. This process alone really refreshes you. Your facial skin and muscle areas are then massaged with essential oils which leave your skin revitalised and gleaming.

You are now treated to a paraffin wax pedicure - a foot and leg treatment that soothes away the tiredness, pressure and tension of overworked limbs. You'll become a pedicure enthusiast after you've experienced this therapy. It's completely relaxing!

Finally, you are invited into the hair salon for a wet cut. The same as the girls, you are encouraged to discuss any hair 'problems' or style frustrations you have, which we'll be pleased to help you solve.

What's the normal cost of a treatment package like this for women and men? You would normally have to pay £79.50. But because you are a (name of bank) staff member you can have the whole package for just £24. **Yes - just £24!**

If you are wondering why I am willing to give this expensive treatment away for so little, here's the reason. I bank at (name of bank). Every time I come into your branch everyone is always so friendly and helpful, which is often, unfortunately, a missing ingredient in today's fast moving business environment. So I thought it would be a nice gesture to offer you a special package that will really help to get you relaxed and feeling great - at a price no one else can possibly get. I hope you agree it's a great offer.

One more thing. **It's important.**

I want you to be completely satisfied with your treatment. So if, for any reason at all, you don't agree it's the most relaxing, invigorating, stimulating and renewing therapy you can experience, if you are disappointed in any way with the tremendous results you will feel with this treatment **then I don't want you to pay for it.** So, at the end of your treatment, if you are not totally happy with what we have given you, just say so and we won't charge you even the considerably reduced cost of just £24.

Can I be any fairer than that? **But hurry** - I can only keep this offer open until Saturday 29th March. So pick-up the phone and book today on (telephone number). Just say you are booking the special (name of bank) offer. I guarantee you'll feel more relaxed and energised than ever before.

Warmly

Cheryl Catland

P.S. I have also arranged a second special offer for you or a friend! I'll give you a voucher for it when you come in for your special treatment.

NAME OF COMPANY
ADDRESS, TELEPHONE

Page 2

Original Copy Centre

ADDRESS, TELEPHONE, FAX

Monday, 2.30pm

Dear Printer,

Have you any copying jobs that you cannot do yourself?
Are you sometimes too busy to cope?

We all know what it's like! You would like to cope with the volume because it's good business and it's **more profit in your bank** every month. But often you just haven't got the time or facilities, right?

Make more money now - and every month!

You can now make **large extra profits** every month by saying 'YES' to this work! Let us do the donkey work, and you make the profit when you charge your customer.

How? We have high-speed, high volume copy machines with in-house engineers to produce all your work to the highest quality. We are able to supply your copy at **extremely low cost** leaving you high margins for profit every time. (See enclosed trade price list for examples!)

And for any jobs you need urgently, we work evenings and weekends. Collection and delivery can also be arranged.

Why *print* short runs, multi-page documents, reports etc.? Let us handle this work for you. It's easier, faster, and **more profitable for you.** You are also assured that our service is completely confidential. We respect your client relationship *at all times* and work is taken on in the *strictest confidence.*

Find out now

Start making **more profit NOW** by using us for all your copying requirements, large and small volumes.

PHONE TODAY for immediate quotes and details of our fast turnaround service! We look forward to your call and to doing business together.

Yours faithfully,

Colin Tewari

P.S. We also provide drilling, binding, stapling, booklet making etc. plus **free machine collating.** We do not undertake printing or design work. Phone **now** for immediate quotes!

The letter, and the one on the next page, has kept my client busy - and highly profitable - for nearly ten years

Original Copy Centre

ADDRESS, TELEPHONE, FAX

Monday, 2.30pm

Dear Business Owner or Director,

Announcing 1/2 price* high quality copying with latest high-speed machines...

How many times do you need duplicated reports, manuals, documents, price lists - even publicity and mailing literature?

When you do, you want them fast, of high quality and at the lowest price you can find.

Armed with the latest high-technology, high-speed copying machines **Original Copy Centre** has your answer. No matter what you want produced, we provide fast turnaround, highest quality copying at prices so low you'll have to look twice.

Your copy professionally finished to your choice

You can choose from a wide variety of finishing to make your copy look its best - binding, stapling, booklet-making, and drilling to name a few - all with **FREE** machine collating! And if you want your work collected and delivered, we do this for you without charge.

You'll find our price list enclosed - please take a look. As you can see, all our charges are **1/2 the usual copying price* or less!**

Have you got a copying requirement now or in the future? **Call us NOW** for an immediate quote, on the number above.

We welcome the possibility of providing you with a copy service - it's what we do well, any quantity big or small. We GUARANTEE you'll be impressed and look forward to receiving your call!

Yours faithfully,

Colin Tewari

P.S. We provide money-saving copying for many businesses near you. Just call, and I'll be pleased to give you their names as references.

*As compared to the majority of copy shops throughout the UK

The letter was sent to every business in my client's catchment area and produced big results

When a client in the dry cleaning business asked me what he could do to increase sales, I advised him to start *regularly communicating with his existing customers*.

The letter I wrote for his first mailing offered customers an introductory Scotchgard™ stain protection treatment for clothes. The idea was to impress as many people as possible with the treatment, which is highly effective. A good percentage of them would then *buy* Scotchgard™ protection in the future.

The letter pulled a 7.2% response and resulted in profitable Scotchgard™ orders soon afterwards. (See letter on page 136.)

Letter #7

Selling computers and providing maintenance and service contracts for company's with I.T. (Information Technology) equipment has become fiercely competitive.

Because computer and office equipment prices have tumbled and continue to do so, the explosion in I.T. buying has led to the birth of *thousands* of PC companies competing on price. **How does any one company gain competitive advantage?**

Tim Leese of Timtype Business Systems (TBS) approached me wanting to increase his maintenance contract business. He started TBS seventeen years ago selling typewriters. When PC's became more affordable he was quick to realise the new potential and started making and selling high quality business computers and providing on-site maintenance and service contracts.

Whereas to begin with he was one of only a handful of such providers, today he's up against *dozens* of companies competing for the same business in any one area. But most of them compete in the same way. *How can you expect to attract more business than your competitors if you market yourself in very much the same ways your competitors do?*

When you realise most businesses promote themselves using the same one or two main marketing methods everyone else in their category uses, it is not difficult to gain immediate advantage by approaching your prospects by a different method.

This is what I suggested TBS do.

To win large maintenance contracts you have to bid for

them. Companies announce their up-coming maintenance requirements by advertising and inviting PC companies to tender for the business. Most service companies *wait* until these announcements are made.

I advised TBS *not* to wait. By becoming *pro-active* instead of *re*active they would steal the thunder from other companies. It sounds logical but most businesses don't do it. Or they do it so badly it has little effect.

We sent a 3-page letter to 2,000 companies explaining how they could benefit by buying a TBS service contract. We included a reply/fax form inviting companies to receive a free quotation; and a reply-paid envelope.

Within six weeks the letter had generated new sales sufficient to boost TBS's turnover by 31 percent.

Cost to print and mail? Under £600.

I have reproduced the letter for you on pages 137—139.

COMPANY NAME
ADDRESS & TELEPHONE

\<1Contact>
\<2Address_1>
\<3Address_2>
\<4Address_3>
\<5City>
\<6County>
\<7Postcode>

Never allow milk, coffee or gravy to stain your clothes again... Here's a FREE introductory stain protection treatment!

Dear Mrs James,

It always happens at the most awkward times, doesn't it? You've got your Sunday best on, or you're just about to go out in a new outfit, and it happens. You spill gravy on your lap. Or coffee goes all over you. Or milk splashes on your silk blouse.

And the stain never properly comes out.

But now you never need worry about every day stains again. What's better, we've arranged to give you an introductory stain protection FREE!

Here's why.

You are a valued customer of ours, so we were thinking what we could give you as a 'thank you'. What better gift than to help you protect your clothes against nasty stains?

How can we afford to give it to you free? Simply because it's the most effective stain protection system and we think *once you've tried it free you'll probably want to use it all the time.* It doesn't cost too much. And it's **really** effective.

The new Scotchgard™ Clothes Protection system means **stains have no chance.** You will not know your clothes have been protected - you can't see anything, or feel any difference. Yet this professional process will protect you against the nastiest of stains, plus make your clothes waterproof, and keep them looking brand new longer.

Come along and try it - FREE! Just bring along a ladies or gents 2-piece suit to be dry cleaned (or a jacket and a pair of trousers) at our normal low charge of £6.10, and we'll give them a Scotchgard™ treatment completely free of charge, worth £2.50.

Bring the enclosed FREE TRIAL VOUCHER. **But hurry - offer must end 16th August.**

Yours sincerely,

Keith Dell

Keith Dell

P.S. Your clothes will even be protected from grease and mud. Best of all, Scotchgard™ does not affect the look or feel of the fabric whatsoever, or its 'breathing' ability. Hurry for your free Scotchgard™ treatment!

A 7.2% response from this letter introduced many customers to Scotchgard™

TBS
TIMTYPE
BUSINESS
SERVICES

Do You Want To <u>Lower</u> Your I.T. Maintenance Costs <u>This</u> Year?

Here's How You Can Start Saving Immediately...

Dear Mr Jantzen,

If you have a high number of computers, printers, or faxes in your organisation TBS can help you reduce the cost of maintaining them.

Because it is vital that all your office machines are kept in reliable working order every day of the year, we provide a fast call-out... *yet much lower cost*... alternative on-site maintenance facility.

More and more big organisations like yours are deciding to use this service to keep their offices running smoothly without needing the big budgets they've been used to in the past.

Our latest, lower-cost maintenance facilities can start saving you money immediately.

<u>Here's how.</u>

With enough machines, you pay just **£39 a year for any PC including Pentiums, £42 for laser printers, £32 for desktop faxes, and £42 for laser faxes.** (These prices can be lower still depending on the quantity of machines you have.)

These prices *include* call-out to your premises **plus** any part your machine needs **plus** fitting. <u>You pay no more, no matter how serious the fault - or how many times you need to call us out during the year.</u>

When you compare these new low prices with any traditional service you might be using at the moment, you can see how expensive it can get <u>not</u> to have a TBS maintenance facility.

And if you don't have a maintenance contract at all, just <u>one</u> individual call-out and replacement part can cost more than a whole year's coverage.

But that's not all you get. Consider how these added benefits will make your life easier...

Page 1. *The letter that increased a PC company's turnover by 31% in six weeks*

- All our engineers are highly qualified specialists. When you call us out you can rest assured your machine is in the hands of an expert.

- Every repair and replacement on your machine is guaranteed. You never need spend another penny on your office machines all year long.

- 81% or repairs are completed in just one visit. If ever your repair can't be completed on the spot, a second fast-return visit by one of our engineers will finish the job. Alternatively we can take your machine away for repair, in which case we will always provide you with a free loan machine in the interim.

If you're wondering how we can keep the price you pay so low, yet realistically maintain a very high standard of service, the answer is straightforward.

TBS provides office machinery maintenance to a large number of businesses, big, medium and small. Some of our better known clients include **Air Canada, Guinness, American Embassy, U.S. Navy, and Lowndes Lambert.** At the other end of the scale we service numerous independents - one to six people businesses. And then many in between.

It's because of this that we can give you the benefit of low cost.

We can buy parts competitively. Our engineers are on the road already, somewhere near you. We have years of experience that have taught us how to diagnose and repair your machine's fault quickly and reliably. **All this keeps our cost down - *and yours too.***

One more thing. **It's important.**

I know your time is valuable. When your office machine breaks down you want an engineer to come out to you fast and complete the repair with the very least interruption to your day.

So I am going to make you this guarantee.

Whenever you need to call us, I guarantee we'll have an engineer out to you normally after just 4 hours of your call, and within a very maximum of 12 working hours.

What's more, if ever we are unable to keep to this guarantee **I will pay you £25 for each time we fail.**

That is how much I respect your time - and how confident I am that we can provide you with a maintenance facility that I think is the best-value you'll find anywhere.

On this guaranteed low-cost, fast-response basis phone now on

01895 270351 or 01895 259564, or return the enclosed reply card for a free, firm quote, and take advantage of our new maintenance facility immediately.

I look forward to keeping your office working 100% reliably, every day of the year.

Yours sincerely,

Tim Leese

P.S. With your local authority financial year ending very soon, why not review your current maintenance agreements. They are almost certainly more expensive. You can change your agreement to a new, low-cost, fast-service guaranteed TBS facility 'instantly'. With local government funds more stringent than ever, every £10 you save helps you. **I believe I can help you make real savings.**

P.P.S. If you are taking the risk that your office machines will not break down, why risk another whole year of potential high call-out and repair costs when you can now have such a low-cost full maintenance facility. Reply today - and take the risk of annoying machines break-downs and unnecessary expense out of your working day.

IBM Accredited Engineers. **Lex Mark** & **Smith Corona** Authorised Service Centre. **Epson** Trained Engineers. **Microsoft** Educational Authorised Reseller. **Hewlett Packard** Authorised Reseller

Page 3

CHAPTER 14

Increase Response
To Sales Letters
Up To 300%!

Does your prospect read your sales letter from salutation to signature, **in the order you wrote it?** Are **indented** paragraphs easier to read than flush left? Do readers retain what you say in **long** sentences more than they do in **short** sentences?

To any entrepreneur, director, or professional seriously interested in optimizing their sales, knowing what makes customers respond is a gold mine of opportunity.

The answers to the above questions by the way are: not usually; yes; no.

Including a P.S. In Your Letters Increases Response Up To 300%

Tests tracking in what order most readers look at a letter reveal some surprising facts:

First: Readers glance at your **headline.**

Second: They turn to your **signature.**

Third: They read your **P.S.** (Post Script.)

Fourth: They read the **body copy** of your letter <u>if</u> they are compelled and interested by your headline, signature, and P.S.

If you fail to capture a readers attention by this stage, they bin your letter.

The P.S. therefore acts as a second headline and is very nearly as important to the success of your letter.

The P.S. is often a *deciding factor* in whether a prospect will bother reading the rest of the letter. If you 'hook' prospects into your offer in the P.S. they are far more likely to read your full letter. If the P.S. doesn't hook them, many will bin it.

A compelling P.S. will generate up to **300 percent more response** to your sales letters.

Seven Types Of P.S. That Increase Response

There are seven types of P.S. that hook your reader most effectively:

1.   **Repeat the main benefit or advantage of your offer.**

In one, two or three short sentences, restate the main benefit or advantage of your offer to peak your readers interest, curiosity, or need.

If you were selling three-piece suites, and you were selling on **quality,** your *benefit or advantage* P.S. could be:

P.S. When you buy a *Bentley Three-Piece Suite,* you buy a lifetime of luxurious comfort and body support, contoured to relax your limbs and support your back — guaranteed for ten years.

Or, if you were selling on **price,** your *benefit or advantage* P.S. could be:

P.S. Buy this £2,500 three-piece suit for just £999... a comforting 60% saving! Don't miss the biggest reductions ever offered by Bentley!

Or, if you were selling on service, your *benefit or advantage* P.S. could be:

P.S. You'll not only have your new 3-piece suite delivered free, but our experienced delivery staff will carefully unpack, check and position your suite anywhere you would like it in your home. **And,** if at any time during the next ten years your suite needs a joint tightened, or if a spring needs replacing, or any of the upholstery has lifted, we will be pleased to correct it free of charge.

2.   Restate your risk-reversal/guarantee

P.S. Remember — when you buy the Bentley 3-Piece Suite you have a full 90-days to decide whether it is the best, most comfortable suite you can own. If you do not agree the Bentley Suite is the most luxurious in seating comfort, simply let us know, and we will arrange a full, 100% refund immediately. No questions.

3.   Compel your prospect to act now

If your prospect does not take action **immediately** the likelihood they will respond sometime in the future *plummets.*

What type of action you want them to take will depend on your offer. You might want prospects to **order directly, arrange an appointment, ask for a sample or demonstration, request a brochure, go into a store, call for more details, etc.**

Whatever action you want you must motivate prospects to take it *now.*

Here are three examples:

P.S. To arrange your free 90-day home trial of the Bentley 3-Piece Suite call 0800 000 000 now! But hurry — stocks of this luxurious suite are limited, so we have to accept free trials on a first-come, first-serve basis.

Or,

P.S. We have only been able to take delivery of 100 luxurious Bentley 3-Piece Suites. Unfortunately when they have been sold we cannot accept further orders. Order today to guarantee delivery!

4.   Add more value

P.S. When you order before 16th April we will add our 5-year upholstery maintenance service **free of charge** (worth £49 per year) to provide you with lasting, luxurious comfort. We'll fully clean your upholstery once a year, and if any area requires mending, we'll repair it 'invisibly' for you.

P.S. The first thing that normally wears on a suite — even a high quality one like the Bentley — are the seat cushions. So any time up to five years after your purchase, we'll come to your home at your request and refill and refurbish your cushions **completely free of charge.** But you must order before April 16th to qualify. Telephone 0800 000 000 and place your order today!

5.   Introduce an unexpected bonus

P.S. If you buy before April 16th we will give you a plush foot stool, in the upholstery you have chosen, worth £217 — completely free of charge.

P.S. FREE ADDITIONAL ITEM! The powerful SuperVac hand-held vacuum and brush set is invaluable to keep your suite looking new for years. It sells for £69.99... but is yours free if you order before March 12th!

6.   Reinforce your price

P.S. The luxurious Bentley Suite is not cheap. But it will offer you a *lifetime* of incomparable comfort, backed up by our 90-day no-risk home trial and no-quibble, 25-year guarantee.

P.S. Our 60% OFF sale ends in 15 days, on 27th March. After that we have to charge the normal higher price. Don't miss out — order right now! Remember, you are protected by our double, 90-day, 100% money-back guarantee, so you can order without any risk.

7. Remind business buyers that your product or service is tax deductible

P.S. Remember, your fee for the *"Out-Sell, Out-Market, Out-Promote, Out-Advertise"* seminar is fully tax-deductible. You can pay in 8 easy-instalments by cheque or credit card. But hurry — only 200 seats available.

P.S. The £99 for Small Business Accounts Software is fully tax-deductible. Start your new, easier PC accounts system off on the right foot! You'll receive your software within 24-hours. Order now!

NOTE: always check with your accountant before claiming your offer is tax deductible.

Never send another sales letter without a compelling P.S. If you have already been using a P.S. in your letters constantly work to make them more compelling.

If you haven't until now realised the importance of the post-script (join the club!) watch your sales improve dramatically as you become increasingly fluent at writing a winning P.S.

CHAPTER 15

How To Out-Advertise Every One of Your Competitors

It is not unusual for a business to spend 10-20 percent of their sales income on advertising. Many mail-order companies plough back up to 50 percent.

So you'd think these businesses would do everything in their power to garner maximum response from every advertising pound. But not one in twenty ads I see stand a chance of pulling maximum response. Why? Because they do not target their prospects accurately, grab prospects attention effectively, lure readers into the ad with interesting copy, or ask the reader to take action.

Well-meaning advertising salespeople sell businesses the *need* to advertise. Companies often see advertising as a way to keep their business name in front of customers, but don't necessarily expect to generate sales from it.

One business owner in the replacement kitchen business said to me, "I have to advertise to keep my name out there, but I don't expect people to call me from my ad!"

Giant companies like car, food and sports manufacturers, guided by advertising agencies who win client praise and industry awards for 'creative' design, not direct sales, waste countless millions on *image* advertising.

How To Make Every Advertising Pound Generate Profitable Sales

I instruct my clients: if you cannot track and measure the response of any piece of marketing, and prove it is generating profitable sales, **stop doing it.**

Every pound you spend on marketing should be forced to *justify* itself. Think about it. You would not spend money on a new tyre if it came with a puncture and didn't inflate. You wouldn't invest in a unit trust if you weren't pretty darn sure it would bring you a good return on your investment.

So why invest in a marketing strategy that cannot track and prove it is producing profitable new sales?

Of course, you *can* produce direct and hugely profitable sales from your advertising.

How To Make Small Ads Pay

Most products and services require *as much advertising space as possible* within reason, usually up to a maximum of one full page. Why? Because:

The more you tell, the more you sell

When you tell the whole sales story you generate dramatically higher response. (See Chapters 7.)

But you **can** effectively sell from small ads too. When you *have* to run small ads because your initial budget is limited, there are strategies you can use to increase response substantially.

10 Winning Techniques To Make Small Ads Pay

1. Use a condensed version of the 7-Step Formula I gave you in Chapter 6, the **A.I.D.A.** formula:

   A = Attention
   Get attention with a compelling headline.

   I = Interest
   Immediately capture your reader's interest by following through on the promise, benefit, or

advantage made in the headline, with details
of your offer.

D = Desire
Create desire in your reader to 'own' your product
or service. How will it benefit your prospect *now?*

A = Action
Ask your reader to *respond now* and provide a
believable reason why they should.

2.   Make the headline as large as possible, up to
     1/3 or even 1/2 the size of your ad. Remember,
     the **headline is 90 percent of the reason prospects
     will be drawn to your offer.**

3.   Use one or two word headlines if you can. For
     example, the headline: **Do you suffer from short
     sight?** can be reduced to:

SHORT
SIGHTED?

4.   Write an 'ideal' ad first—a half or full page ad,
     or a sales letter—then use the *very essence* of your
     sales message to create a small ad.

5.   Use *telegram* language. For example, the sentence,
     "We will be pleased to send you a copy of our free
     booklet" can be condensed to, "Free booklet."

6.   Use small type, down to 6-point, or even 5-point
     so that you can fit more copy in. (Unless you are
     targeting older people who may appreciate larger
     type, minimum 8-point.)

7.   Test whether you attract more response *with* or

without an illustration or picture of your product or service. Including an illustration or picture does **not** necessarily increase response. You will often find utilising your space with good copy will out-pull space used for a graphic.

8. Use a freephone number — response will increase between 10 - 30 percent.

9. Write your ad to look and read **more like an editorial** than an advert. Often something that *looks* like editorial will attract more readership and response than something that is blatantly an advert.

    People inherently dislike and often distrust advertising, unless they are specifically looking for something. But they are naturally drawn to *news*. Create 'news-type' headlines (see Chapter 5.) For instance:

SHORT
SIGHT
CURE
DISCOVERED

or:

NEW CAR
DOES
76 MILES TO
GALLON

or:

PRICES

TUMBLE
ON MEN'S
SUITS

10. Offer a free information pack, booklet, special report, or sample. Your response will increase.

How To Measure The Effectiveness of Your Adverts

Track the response you get from each ad. How? Include a *key* that tells you which ad, in which publication the response comes from. For instance, if you were advertising in the Sunday Times on 26th April, you could say: Write to ABC Company, Dept ST264, Address. ST stands for Sunday Times, 264 stands for the 26th day of the fourth month, April.

You can use any code you wish. The importance is that you track response *accurately*. You can then test one ad against another to find out which appeal is pulling most response (See Chapter 18.)

Examples of Winning Small Ads

Winning Small Ad #1

I wrote the ad at the top of page 150 for a small hair salon that was having difficulty attracting new clients for their new stylist. The ad produced 61 new customers in three days.

Around half of the people who paid £2 on their first visit became fully paying clients after their second visit.

Winning Small Ad #2

This ad (bottom of page 150) and four similar versions of it, produced a constant stream of profitable business for over five years. In this case I found the illustration of the guitar player increased response by over 30 percent.

continued on page 152...

100 HAIR CUTS
for just £2 EACH by professional stylist

YES! You can have a professional hair cut for just £2! No catches. No hidden small print.

Why are we giving away 100 hair cuts, at such low cost?

Simply because we want to introduce you to our newest recruit... professional stylist, **Keeley Honnor.**

We know once you've had your hair cut by her, you'll be impressed by her skilful styling and almost certainly want to keep coming back to her.

Girls and guys accepted!

100%   Money-Back Guarantee

Keeley is a professional hair stylist. Her cutting is impressive. But we want <u>you</u> to be 100 delighted - even though you're only paying £2. <u>If for any reason you are not 100% pleased with your cut, you can walk away and not owe us a penny.</u> No questions asked.

But hurry... first 100 people only. Phone now to book your special £2 hair cut!

01227 000 000
(New clients only)

This 5 x 2 ad produced 61 new customers in three days for a hair salon

BE A SUCCESSFUL LEAD GUITARIST

Make money playing while you are still learning

FREE Cassette shows you how!

With the unique Rockmaster Method you can learn exciting lead and rhythm playing to rock band standard after just 3 lessons!! INCREDIBLE BUT TRUE!! You could join a money-earning band just weeks after starting the program!!!

Guaranteed fastest learning method known today.

Send today for free Rockmaster pamphlet and details of unique FREE 21-day trial offer.

ROCKMASTER PUBLICATIONS, 64 W.M.P. (Box 117), High Wycombe, Bucks HP10 0EZ.

This ad kept on pulling a profitable response for over 5 years

"Why Some People Almost Always Get a Well Paid Job"

Some people seem to get lucky when they go for interviews, and apply for well paid jobs.

Why?

Because they have the extra office skills that employers are looking for... and expecting... today. Now you can get 'lucky' too! The latest **guaranteed career courses** train you for a successful, well paid job.

You can now take inten-sive, guaranteed courses in:

- Word Processing
- Book-keeping
- Typing
- Shorthand up to R.S.A. level

How do you know you'll succeed? We GUARANTEE a **100% PASS RATE** — or your money back. Phone NOW for FREE information pack, no obligation. But *hurry* before places are filled in the busy September period.

FREEPHONE 0800 000 000

COMPANY NAME AND ADDRESS

This headline outpulled every other tested. The advert produced 400% increase in response

MUMS..
WANT TO GET BACK TO WORK?

Have you been away from work raising your family? Want to restart your career? You can! Find out today how easy it now is. A low-cost New Career Course brings you up to date with Word Processing, Typing, PC Skills, Shorthand, Book-Keeping, etc. Learn the skills you need to get back to work, with these quick and easy RSA Diploma courses.

SEE IF IT'S FOR YOU

Take advantage of a free trial lesson to choose which course suits you best... without any obligation. Don't delay your new career any longer. Phone now for free info on freephone: 0800-000-000 and ask for RS1 New Career Pack. Office Career College, High St, England

The MUMS headline and body copy generated good volumes of targeted response. Do you think it would have responded as well with a different headline?

24-Hour Curtain Cleaning
FREE collection & re-hanging

Have your curtains collected, cleaned and rehung in 24-Hours!

- FREE take-down and re-hang service
- Guaranteed 24-hour service no extra cost
- Your satisfaction guaranteed <u>or we reclean free</u>
- Includes Drapes, Austrians, Swags and Tails

"There's no one that cleans curtains like Butlers"
Book your curtain cleaning today on 0800 000 000

BUTLERS CLEANING

Tell people precisely what benefit or advantage they will get by buying from you. This ad produced good business for a dry cleaner

The free information pack consisted of the letter on page 128, a glossy brochure, enrolment form, and reply paid envelope.

Winning Small Ad #3

The ad with the headline **"Why Some People Almost Always Get a Better Paid Job"** (page 151) out-pulled every other headline tested against it. It increased my clients response by 400 percent compared with the ad she was using beforehand.

Winning Small Ad #4

The **MUMS** ad (page 151) was aimed at... **mums** who might want to resume their career with updated skills, or start a new career. It out-pulled others tested against it.

Winning Small Ad #5

By focusing on their main selling benefit — fast turnaround — this curtain cleaning company attracted more customers. Note the emphasis on *great* service; free take-down and re-hang service, and a free re-clean if customers are not completely satisfied. Is it surprising this ad produces profitable response?

How To Make Big Ads Pay

Prospects do not want to read long copy in advertisements, right?
Wrong.
More people read ads with long copy than ads with short copy. Why? Because customers are screaming for *facts* about what they want to buy. Without the relevant facts about competing brands, or products, or services, how can a customer intelligently *decide* which is the best purchase to make?
Most companies make it *difficult* to decide because they do not give anywhere near the amount of information about their product or service the customer needs.
My personal experience is that long copy out-pulls short copy nearly **every time.** The founding Father of modern adver-

tising, Claude C Hopkins, coined the phrase *The more you tell, the more you sell*. He said, "It has never failed to prove so in any test we know."

Why Car Advertisements Frustrate The Heck Out of Me!

Do car manufacturers think the public is *stupid?* They show us glitzy 'creative' commercials that cumulatively cost *tens of millions of pounds* that tell us little or nothing about the fundamental benefits and advantages of buying *their* make of car.

Do they — and the advertising agencies who create their commercials — seriously expect large numbers of us to run to our nearest car dealer and buy their model on the basis that they've shown us a pretty person driving a pretty-coloured car in pretty countryside? BS!

If car manufacturers provided solid, interesting, educational, compelling **facts** about the benefits of their models, they would discover it takes *far less money* attracting *more customers* than image advertising can.

One Car Manufacturer Leading The Way

You may or may not like their style but you'll take your hat off to their marketing expertise.

Daewoo Cars seem to have appeared from nowhere and become a major player in the UK auto market. How did they do it? First they had a good product with clear-cut advantages, price being one of them. But their high sales rise has been achieved by no-messing, sleeves-up, information-filled, benefit-oriented advertising that explains *why you should buy a Daewoo*. Many thousands now do and Daewoo are carving a stronger position in the market every year.

Why don't other car manufacturers sit up and take note?

Fill Your Big Ad With Long, Interesting Copy

The most words ever used in a single page advertisement (to my knowledge) is 6,540. The ad appeared in the *New York Times* by the Investment company Merrill Lynch. **One insertion** pulled **10,000 responses!** for a booklet titled, "How To Invest."

If, or as soon as, you have the budget to test big ads, fill them with long, interesting, relevant copy. Provide your prospects with the factual and compelling knowledge they need to make an educated buying decision. They will appreciate it. And they'll buy in far *greater volumes.*

10 Winning Techniques To Make Big Ads Pay

1. Always use a heavily benefit-oriented headline. Never use just the name of your product or service, and *never* put your company name at the top (See Chapter 5.)

2. Test whether you get greater response *with* or *without* a picture of your product.

An illustration of the product does not automatically attract more response. The longest running advert ever recorded — over 40 years — consists of one full page of text only. The headline is: **Do You Make These Mistakes in English?**

3. Always place a *caption* under your illustrations. Like a P.S. in a letter, captions get high readership. Use your captions as another *selling opportunity.*

For example, if you were advertising a new car, and you wrote a caption for beneath the photograph, don't simply say:

The new SI700

Instead, give prospects a **selling benefit** like:

The new SI700 — independent tests show it to be the safest car on the road

or,
*So quiet you can't hear the engine
running – the luxurious new SI700*

4.   If you show your product, always show it **in use.**
     Tests prove customers respond more to products
     in use than products shown statically.

5.   Always have people in your ads looking **directly
     at the reader.** Customers are drawn more to eye-
     contact than by a person looking away.

6.   Provide sufficient **proof** that the claims you
     make about your product or service are true.
     Use **anecdotal endorsements** (see Chapter 6)
     and **reasons-why** (see Chapter 8.)

7.   Make your ad 'look' less like an advert and
     more like an **editorial.**

In most cases, people like *news* more than they like adverts.
Adverts are on the whole only searched by prospects actively
looking for something to buy. So you will attract those anyway.

But people always have interests and needs and desires that
they are not *actively* searching to fulfil. When you make your
advert appear more like newsworthy editorial you attract more of
those prospects too.

8.   Break your copy up with interesting or curious
     sub-headlines that lead your reader into the next
     block of copy. This makes your ad much *easier* to
     read. The easier you make it for people to read,
     the more *will* read it.

9.   Always place your ad on a **right hand** page in the
     first third of the paper or magazine. Any deviation
     from these positions produces measurably less
     response.

The best position is on the *immediate* right hand pages — page 1, 3, 5, 7. You'll often have to pay a premium to get on these pages but if you have a good ad, the premium will be paid for a number of times over by the additional response you receive.

As a general rule, the earlier right hand page you can get on the more response you'll receive. But if early pages are unavailable you should still get good response on a right-hand page within the **first third of the publication.** If the sales department cannot guarantee a first third position **wait until the next issue to advertise.**

10. Always 'hook' your prospect into your product or service by asking them to take some form of **action** immediately.

How? *Involve them immediately **while you have their attention.*** I see hundreds of big adverts that have cost £20,000-£70,000, interesting a prospect with details of an offer, only to end the ad with a 'cold' message like *at all major PC stores,* or *see your nearest electrical stockist* or some such message.

One rule I have that brings my clients more profit quickly is 'get 'em while they're hot!' You lose a considerable portion of your potential response if you spend big advertising pounds and don't provide interested prospects an opportunity to act immediately and **specifically.**

Motivate prospects to **do *something* now.** For example, if you were selling a new wide-angle TV, at the end of your ad, say:

Interested? Phone freephone 0800 000 000 for a free colour brochure and details of our valuable First-1000-Buyers discount.

Or, *Cut out this special FREE HOME TRIAL coupon and take it to any of the main dealers listed above. They will arrange a no-risk, 10-day home trial for you because you're a* Daily Express *reader! But hurry — only 1,000 free home trials available.*

If your business offers a service — let's say you provide a computer maintenance service — you could say:

Send for the free booklet **21 Simple Ways To Keep Your PC Trouble-Free For Years** *and details of our PC maintenance introductory offer.*

Or, *Phone freephone 0800 000 000 now to receive an 'instant' maintenance quote and details of our fast-response guarantee.*

Do you see how much **more response** you will garner from each advert when you involve your prospect in taking action? (See Chapter 6, Step 7.)

A Proven Design For Big Adverts

The ad on page 158 demonstrates a proven design for large adverts — illustration at the top immediately followed by your headline, or illustration immediately below your headline, followed by interesting details about your offer and a compelling call-to-action your prospect can respond to (see 7-Step Formula, Chapter 6.)

The columns are *narrow* because they are easier to read than wide columns. You will notice newspapers always use narrow columns. Journalism has become expert at knowing how to attract maximum readership. Marketing strategists and copywriters can learn much from seeing how newspapers are laid out, how compelling headlines are constructed and so on.

I've used the copy for the SI700 car examples in Chapter 6 for the ad.

PHOTOGRAPH OF YOUR CAR HERE, PICTURED *IN USE*

The new SI700 - Tested the <u>safest</u> car in it's category

"You are <u>safer</u> in the luxury new 5-seat SI700 than in any other car in its category"

If you need the space of a family saloon, but also want to know you and your passengers are uniquely protected against even a hard impact, the new SI700 saloon will interest you.

What's more, you'll enjoy a level of comfort usually only associated with saloons costing twice the price. Plus you have 27 advanced interior and exterior driving functions electronically controlled at the push of a button to give your drive even more control, comfort *and safety.*

Record-breaking new safety level

When it comes to keeping your family safe in the event of an accident, you want to know no short-cuts have been taken. When the SI700 saloon was on the drawing board, the instruction to our design engineers was, "Build a car that is stronger and safer than anything on the road." It took them five years and six weeks to achieve, but the results have set high new standards for the motor industry.

Solid steel 'cage' protects you

The entire engine and boot compartments are built around a web of solid steel bars that will take an impact of up to 56 miles an hour without distorting the passenger cabin even 1 inch.

The SI700's four doors are fortified against impact with the unique LifeProtect System developed by our engineers. A formidably strong 'H' shaped steel guard in each door locks tight into the door frame when closed to protect you against a side impact of up to 48 miles an hour.

Inside the protected passenger cabin, four airbags are fitted - two in the front, and two stowed in the back of the front seats for your rear passengers.

If this saloon had been available a year ago in England 3,867 serious road injuries could have been avoided. That's the number of passengers injured because their cars did not meet our new, record-high impact standard. As you can see, *we take your safety as seriously as our own.*

Luxurious comfort, sophisticated styling

You might think that a car so focused on safety would lack in comfort and stylish accessories. Not so. When you first sit in an SI700, you'll be surprised by its luxurious feel and sophisticated styling.

Every seat in the cabin supports and secures you and your passengers. But the seats are much more than just seats. In the depth of winter you can heat each seat individually to between 20 - 50 degrees. In the heat of summer, each seat can be air cooled to maximise your comfort.

And - unlike most of our competitors - we do not think one seat fits all. Individual, electronic seat adjustment at the flick of a switch allows you to shape the seat to suit your posture. Not only that, but you can enter your personal adjustment into the seat's memory. Next time you get in the SI700, if someone else has adjusted your seat differently, simply punch the memory and it will readjust.

Experts give it the thumbs-up

It might be said we could be over-enthusiastic about the higher than ever impact protection we've achieved. So to make sure we weren't biased, we took the SI700 along to the Motoring Association for an independent view. Here's what their Chief Safety Engineer said.

"The patented 'H' steel crash bars in every door are a breakthrough in impact protection. We ran five separate side collision tests, and sure enough, in every test the SI700 withstood an impact of up to 48 miles per hour. Any passengers in the car during the impact would have survived largely unscathed."

Other independent sources are astonished at the SI700's safety, too. Which Car? magazine classes the SI700 as, "Extraordinarily safe. There is no other car in its category that will protect you against forceful impact so effectively." Feb 1998.

"Our crash tests revealed the new SI700 saloon to be the safest family saloon on the road." Consumer Choice, Jan 1998.

"I have just gone and bought an SI700 for my wife. Life is too precious to risk destroying in a road accident. The SI700's new safety standards mean I can sleep sounder knowing my wife and family are better protected." Senior Surgeon, Accident & Emergency Department, London Hospital.

Is it worth risking?

If you don't choose the SI700 saloon, will you ever feel quite as safe driving? Really, when it comes to safety, there is now no other choice. You and your family will simply not be as safe in any other car. By a life-saving 43 percent.

To sum it up

In a nutshell, if you are looking for uncompromising safety, in a saloon luxuriously designed for a silent, comfortable driving experience, plus a myriad of additional electronically controlled features normally only found in a car costing twice as much, the new SI700 saloon cannot be compared.

I think you'll also agree the stylish body design does everything to visually impress, while effectively disguising the fortress within.

Free test drive

Find out for yourself how safe - and luxuriously comfortable - the SI700 Saloon is. Simply call Freephone **0800 000 000 to arrange a test drive at your nearest dealer.** Alternatively, ask us to send you the full colour brochure, "Why the SI700 is the safest—and most luxurious—saloon on the road," plus the Automobile Association's special report on the 7 safest saloons on the market.

CHAPTER 16

Chance Discovery Reveals How To Increase Flyer And Insert Response Up To 8-Times

An entrepreneur in the will-writing business phoned me wanting to know if I could help make his flyers profitable.

He told me: *After printing and distribution costs, flyers never produce enough sales to make a profit.*

Most businesses I come across find it difficult making money from flyers. But there's a simple way to multiply response to both flyers and inserts.

Letters Pull More Response Than Flyers

The smartest thing you can do with flyers and inserts is to... change them into letters!

An interesting thing happened a few years ago. A client asked me to write copy for a flyer she wanted to distribute. I wrote and designed the flyer, we tested 1,000 and it brought a decent number of new sales and made a marginal profit.

But I knew that a *letter* might grab people's attention more. So, as a test, I re-set the exact same wording on the flyer onto a one page A4 letter, with a salutation and a signature.

Again we tested 1,000. This time the 'letter' out-pulled the flyer **nearly ten to one.** *Ten times more sales simply by making the sales message look like a letter.*

It proved to me once again the unequivocal **selling power** of letters.

Why Do Letters Work Better?

People pay attention to a *letter* more than any other printed material. Why? Because it is the original and still today the main form of one-to-one communication.

If you receive a letter, it suggests someone has written you a *personal* and *individual* message. So you take notice.

If you receive a standard 'flyer' it suggests a *mass* sales message. So you take less notice, or you bin it without a second thought.

A 'letter' commands:

More immediate attention

So you:

Increase readership of your sales message

and therefore:

Generate higher response

What Size Should Your Letter-Flyer Be?

I prefer A4 size. Why? Because A4 is standard letter size. Any deviation from the 'look' of a letter can be detrimental because it then appears more like a mass promotion.

If you have to fold it to make it easier for your distributors to put through letter boxes, or in the case of inserts, to accommodate a small magazine, fold it so your **headline** is the first thing people see.

Is Any Colour Paper OK?

Not usually. I find the best responding paper colour to be *white*. Again for the same reasons. Traditionally, letters are printed with black ink on white paper and I think people still 'see' a black/white letter as something they should look at.

Your accountant, solicitor, bank manager, mortgage broker, insurance broker writes to you on white paper. White has an air of importance. Stick to white 95 percent of the time and you can't go wrong.

What Should Be Included On a Flyer Or Insert?

Write a flyer or insert just a you would a sales letter. Tell as much of the full sales story as possible. Use the 7-Step Formula in Chapter 6 to grab reader's attention, interest them in your offer, and lead them through to responding now.

Example Letter-Flyers That Pull Big Response

Here are two flyers that I rewrote as letter-flyers and saw response soar.

Letter-Flyer #1
This was written for a client in the building trade. I became fascinated in working with them when they showed me a new building material called *Renothane* that was so strong and durable it could be used to instal any floor, flat roof, or driveway — without ever needing maintenance, for life!

The flyer on page 162 is typically what this company would send out to produce leads. Response? Very low.

The letter you see on pages 163-164 is the 'letter-flyer' I wrote to test a cold distribution to general house-owners. We tested 2,500 and received a promising response — £1,600 sales.

Next we rolled out with 10,000 distribution and got over £8,000 new sales, at a printing and distribution cost of less than £650. That's enough proof to roll-out the letter on a larger scale

continued on page 167...

161

FLAT ROOFS.. FLOORS.. DRIVEWAYS

Amazing new building material saves you £100's of pounds!

A new building material just obtained saves you money, and means no maintenance for life! We can put in a new floor, a new flat roof, or a driveway that will look great, is completely waterproof, and strong enough to not need maintenance for years.

We are currently looking for a limited number of homes in <u>your area</u> to feature in our new brochure. We can therefore offer 25% discount on your floor, flat roof, or driveway. But hurry — you must respond before March 27th to qualify.

To find out more, or to book a no-obligation quote,

Call free now on:

0800 731 7633

KB CHEMICALS LTD
HAMILTON LODGE, CRANES LANE, KELVEDON, ESSEX CO5 9AX
TEL: 0800 731 7633   FAX: 01376 573424

The typical type of flyer this building company would use.
It will not pull as much response as a 'letter'

IMPORTANT ANNOUNCEMENT FOR THE OWNER OF THE HOUSE IN WITHAM

"If you are thinking of having a new floor, flat roof, or new driveway, this information can save you a lot of money"

10:42, Monday

Dear Witham House Owner,

Until seven months ago, if you wanted a new floor, flat roof, or even a new driveway you were limited to the standard materials used by the building trade. Nearly all of them produced good results but they were expensive.

Now, thanks to a remarkable new material that is strong as steel, flexible, non-slip, retains its full colour even after decades, and lasts for life, you can save a considerable amount of money on improving your home.

Professional contractors are calling it a 'miracle' material. What's it called? RENOTHANE. It's a way to floor any room in your house, seal a flat roof 100% watertight for life, or install a driveway that looks exactly like high quality Tarmac or attractive gravel that lasts for life without maintenance.

Here are the 3 ways you can use Renothane to enhance your home:

1.   Install non-slip flooring in your bathroom, shower, or kitchen. Because Renothane comes in 32 different finishes, you can now have a beautiful looking floor to enhance your room, that is also completely non-slip. What's more, Renothane is 100% waterproof, ideal for bathrooms, showers, and kitchens.

It can be finished as smooth as marble, or textured to give it an attractive carpet-like finish. Your floor can be made to look traditional, modern, or even 'sporty.'

To have a Renothane floor in your bathroom, shower, or kitchen costs only £28 per square metre. What's more, you can now save 25% - down to £21 per square metre, and it's guaranteed for life. See no-risk guarantee over page.

2.   Seal your flat roof watertight for life. Until now flat roofs have been a problem. As you know if you've got one, they need regular resurfacing usually every 5 - 7 years to stop water from leaking through. And you can't walk on them without risking damaging the tar and felt surface.

Now... because Renothane is as strong as steel plate and 100% watertight no matter how many times you walk on it... flat roof maintenance is a problem of the past. Even better, you won't be able to tell the difference between a Renothane flat roof and a normal tar and felt roof. Renothane looks exactly the same - or it can be made any other colour and finish you want at no extra cost.

What's the cost? Just £28 per square metre - minus your 25% saving. Again, you are given a life guarantee with a Renothane flat roof - see over page.

3.   You can now have a beautiful Tarmac-looking, or gravel-looking driveway that will last for life without any maintenance. If you've looked into having a Tarmac or gravel driveway, you'll know they both need regular, two or three-yearly maintenance to

Please turn over...

Letter-Flyer — Page 1.

When my client tested this A4 size letter-flyer it generated over £8,000 new sales, at a cost of £640

keep them looking good.

But now you can have a Renothane driveway that looks and feels exactly like black or red Tarmac (or any other colour you want), or just like gravel, <u>that never needs any maintenance at all.</u> Why? Because Renothane is a stone-based polyurethane resin that is about 45 times stronger than epoxy resin. You can drive a 20-ton truck over a 1-inch thick layer of it on a substrate without it even noticing. It's <u>that</u> strong. Even better, a Renothane driveway costs just £35 per square metre.

How you can save money. If you are thinking of having a new floor, flat roof, or driveway put in this spring, you can save a considerable amount of money. Why? Two reasons. **First,** frankly, February and March are normally our quietest months, so we'd rather offer you a discount and keep our employees busy, even though our profit is substantially reduced. But we are only making a discount available to local people (we're based in Kelvedon.) For this reason I am prepared, and happy, to give you <u>a full **25% OFF** any Renothane floor, roof, or driveway</u> during February and March only.

Second, because you will literally never need to redo or repair Renothane for a lifetime, you save the considerable additional maintenance costs of other materials. These can amount to *hundreds of pounds* over the years.

One more thing. **It's important you know this.** I know why contractors are calling Renothane a 'miracle' material. It's shear strength, complete watertight property, and life-lasting endurance makes it better value than any other material you could use. But I want you to see it for yourself and be 100% satisfied too. So I want to give you an unusual, double, 100% guarantee with the work we do for you.

First, if *for any reason whatsoever*, you are not completely delighted with your Renothane floor, flat roof, or driveway when it's been installed.. if you are not satisfied with the way it looks, feels, and enhances your home.. just say so, and I will undo the Renothane that was laid, make good, and not charge you a penny. **There'll be no questions, and no hard feelings on my part, either.** Second, because your Renothane floor, roof, or driveway is guaranteed to last for life without maintenance, if anything at all ever needs repairing, I will do it free, even though you got a full 25% saving.

Obviously, in making you this 100% guarantee, I know how reliable, strong, and completely waterproof Renothane is. The likelihood of you not being delighted with the job I do for you, or ever having any need for maintenance, is very small indeed. <u>Nevertheless, I want you to have the final decision and a life-long guarantee of Renothane's superiority.</u> I hope you agree this is fair.

On this 100%, no-risk basis - and if you want to save a full 25% before March 27th - **phone freephone 0800 731 7633 today to see how good Renothane will look on your floor, flat roof, or driveway, and a free, no-obligation estimate.**

Warmly,

Keith Bennett

Keith Bennett

P.S. You can save a full 25% <u>only until 27th March.</u> Most importantly, because Renothane lasts for life you'll save hundreds of pounds in maintenance costs over the years. It's guaranteed for life! **Phone now for a free, firm estimate at 25% less - freephone 0800 731 7633.**

KB CHEMICALS LTD
HAMILTON LODGE, CRANES LANE, KELVEDON, ESSEX CO5 9AX
TEL: 0800 731 7633   FAX: 01376 573424

Letter-Flyer — Page 2.

HIGHTOWN
DRY CLEANERS

ADDRESS, TELEPHONE, OPENING HOURS

FAST DRY CLEANING AT COMPETITIVE PRICES

- Shirts/blouses £2.95
- Trousers/skirts £2.95
- 2-Piece Suits £6.10
- 3-Piece Suits £8.50
- Jackets £3.95
- Dresses £4.70
- Coats £5.70

Come in today and find out why we dry clean for over 500 local families already. Save 15% with the coupon below!

15% OFF WITH THIS COUPON

This type of flyer is better than nothing but is unlikely to pull maximum response. It produced only a handful of new customers for a dry cleaner

"Why this dry cleaner is ready to give you your first two visits at 1/2 PRICE... and then, for the next 12 months, will do 2 shirts <u>free</u> everytime you bring in two suits and a jacket"

Monday, 2.35pm

Dear Householder,

Yes! It's true. We will give you your first two visits for half price - no matter how much cleaning you bring in.

Then, for the next 12 months, every time you bring in just two suits and a jacket, we'll clean two shirts completely free of charge!

Why are we going to extraordinary lengths to acquire your custom?

Frankly, we have just moved into new premises in the town centre and we want to increase the number of families who use our competitive service. We think that once you've had your dry cleaning done by us once you'll want to stay a customer.

Why? Well, 527 families in this area already use us and tell us they prefer our service because of the special treatment they get at no extra cost.

For instance, on your first visit you'll be given a free dry cleaning zip-bag that you can bring your clothes in each time. It saves you having to use black bags or running in with clothes in your arms.

Second, we return your cleaned and pressed clothes in a strong, waterproof carry bag with a hanger. It's free, and yours to keep and use each time you come in.

Thirdly, you can choose from a variety of useful services to suit your schedule — 1-hour cleaning, 4-hour cleaning, next day cleaning, 8am - 10pm opening hours 7 days a week, 52 weeks a year, door-to-door collection and delivery, low-cost Scotchgard clothes protection, special price reduction offers, and more.

One more thing - it is important you know this. We want you to be 100% satisfied with the high quality dry cleaning and pressing we do for you. If - for any reason whatsoever - you do not agree that every item of clothing we return is dry cleaned to the very highest standard, and that our pressing is sharp and accurate - even in the hardest to press places like underarm, trouser crotches, and pleat folds - simply let us know after you get home, and we will dry clean and/or re-press your clothes again absolutely free.

Come in now with as little or as much cleaning as you have and get it for **half price.** (Remember, your second visit is half price too!) Or call us free on **0800 000 000** and ask us to collect and deliver it for you for just £2.

Warmly,

Chris Hopkins

P.S. Remember - your first two visits HALF PRICE, then two shirts FREE for a whole year with two suits and a jacket. Plus every item is 100% guaranteed for your complete satisfaction, or we re-clean free.

HIGHTOWN DRY CLEANERS
ADDRESS, TELEPHONE, OPENING HOURS

The revamped letter-flyer with a more powerful offer... it pulled 800 percent more response to tens of thousands of homes, which is being done as this book goes to press.

This company can generate tens of thousands of pounds additional, profitable sales simply by changing their flyer to a letter. You can do the same!

Letter-Flyer #2

They work for smaller businesses too! A dry cleaning company was having difficulty maintaining sales during the summer. They had tried distributing 10,000 of the flyer shown on page 165. Although it brought in a handful of new customers, about 10 as I remember (0.1%), it didn't solve their problem of slower summer sales.

I rewrote the offer in letter format (see page 166) and we tested with another 10,000 delivered to homes in their town. This time the flyer attracted 83 new customers in two weeks (0.83%).

Bear in mind the cost of the two flyers were exactly the same — 10,000 printed flyers and 10,000 distributed through letter boxes in both cases. *But one produced 830 percent more response.*

Before You Spend More Money on Glossy Flyers, Test a Letter!

The temptation is to spend more on a glossy image for your business. But time after time, higher cost, full colour glossy flyers fail to pull as much response as a good letter — often by margins as large as 500 - 1,000 percent.

Are you thinking of producing a brochure or catalogue for your products? Do you already have one? Then discover: **How To Multiply Sales From Brochures...**

CHAPTER 17

Revealed: How To Multiply Sales From Brochures

Very few marketing departments or copywriters know how to create a brochure that produces high sales. Yet many businesses would profit by having one. Most brochures fail to generate profitable sales because although brochure design seems straightforward — take good quality photographs, describe what you sell, present it attractively, include your company details — surprisingly, this type of brochure is an expensive luxury.

(By 'brochure' I am referring to anything from a one-page glossy sheet to a multi-page catalogue of products. The method of maximising sales from any of these is the same.)

Here's The Secret

Just like your *letter*, your brochure must tell the *whole sales story*. A brochure, like your letter, is simply...

Salesmanship in Print

You wouldn't send your salesperson out to a prospect only to drop some photographs of your product on his desk and blurt off a list of specifications and stylised sales-hype. No! Your salesperson would take the time and trouble to present your prospect with the whole sales story — the specific benefits, advantages, and reasons-why your offer is of value.

Your brochure must be your salesperson in print.

10 Secrets of Successful Brochure Design

1. You **must** put an attention-getting **headline** on the front cover.
2. Every product you feature should have its own compelling headline.
3. Your copy should be interesting, informative, and educational.
4. You should use only high quality photographs.
5. You should put a **caption** under every photograph or drawing featuring a **selling benefit.**
6. Use only high quality print reproduction.
7. Use only **two different typefaces** throughout, not more. More than two fonts look messy.
8. Always include a **separate letter** signed by the owner, director, or Chairman.
9. Always include a separate or tear-out order form Or in the case of field sales, an appointment form, or booking card.
10. Make your ordering process and instructions easy to follow. (Many ordering instructions I see are so confusing customers simply don't bother trying to figure them out, and simply do not order.)

Examples Brochure Copy That Sells

Here are examples of how to write brochure copy that grabs your readers attention, keeps them riveted to your sales description, and motivates them to order.

Front Cover

If you received two office supplies brochures, one with just the name of the company emblazoned across the top, and another with the headline, **Improve Your Office... Here are The Top 100 Best-Value Office Supplies for Spring,** which one would pique your interest most? The second of course, because it promises an advantage—the top-100 best-value supplies.

Many brochures are never opened, or looked at with much

more than a fleeting glance, because there is no promise of benefit on the cover. The example below shows a redesigned brochure cover with a compelling headline.

Always use a compelling headline on the front cover of your brochure

Facts Don't Sell. Only *Benefits* Sell.

Many brochures simply list *specifications* and *facts* about the company's products. But facts don't sell. Only **benefits** sell. You should bring your brochure **alive** with copy extolling the benefits and advantages of your offer.

Here's how one major office supply store describes a fax machine in their brochure (see page 171, Fig 1).

Now, does this copy excite you? Like heck it does! It's *boring.* With twenty other fax machines on the page of this brochure you have to long-haul yourself through twenty lists of uninteresting *facts.*

Instead, your brochure copy should bring your products

SQ170 TEL/FAX

- Caller ID function
- Answer Machine interface
- Automatic switch between fax/phone calls
- 15 sheet automatic paper feed
- 65 speed dial stations
- Automatic paper cutter
- Complete with 12 months on site warranty

£289

Fig 1. *A list of features is not enough to maximise sales*

Silent Secretary Screens Your Calls—and Files Your Faxes!

Here's the smartest fax you can buy! Acts like a silent secretary. First, it allows you to screen your calls. How? It displays the **name** of the caller on its LED screen. If you're busy—or just on your way out—you see who's calling and decide whether to talk, or let the message pad record the call. Second, it receives faxes *silently.* Even if it's right on your desk, **you'll hardly hear a thing** as it silently prints your fax, cuts it, and stores it neatly in the attached in-tray.

The 'Silent Secretary' Phone/ Fax SQ170—only £289

You'll love these breakthrough functions as you use it!

Until now, faxing was painfully slow. That's now changed. The SQ170 accepts up to 15 pages to fax, reliably faxes them, and stores each page in an 'out' tray. What's more, you press just two buttons to speed dial your message to any one—or all—of 65 people or companies you've preset.

Plus, this machine reliably distinguishes between incoming faxes or messages, just like your best secretary! No more frustrating, non-working tel/fax recognition. This system really works. Handy when you're out of the office, too. Your messages are digitally stored which means you can retrieve them 'instantly' (no waiting for tapes to rewind or fast forward—it's instant!). And your faxes are neatly piled in your in-tray, in order. This fax is the best on the market.

100%, 365-DAY GUARANTEE

Our guarantee is simple and total. If—for any reason—you don't agree the 'Silent Secretary' fax/phone is the most advanced, most silent, and most useful fax on the market, you may simply return it within 365 days and receive a 100% refund, no questions. **Buy this fax today without risk—it's exceptional!**

Advanced features: ●Identifies callers *by name* ●Digital massage pad allows instant access to messages ●Reliably distinguishes between faxes and phone calls ●15 sheet automatic paper feed ●65 speed dial stations ●Automatic paper cutter ●12 months on-site warranty ● 100%, 365-day money-back guarantee of satisfaction, no questions

Fig 2. *Compelling headline plus interesting, informative copy sells more product!*

alive. You should make reading your copy interesting. Figure 2 on page 171 shows the rewritten copy I used.

The sales story takes more space in the brochure but more than makes up for it in multiplied sales. You will also see I have kept the list of specifications. Most people will read the detailed copy. But if a reader prefers skipping right to the specs, he can. That way you increase your chances of appealing to both types of customer — the emotional buyer, and the matter-of-fact buyer.

How To Test The Selling Power Of Your Brochure

As in any other form of marketing, you should test how well your brochure sells your product before you print large quantities. Every change in headline, sub-headline, copy, and design can increase or decrease response — by considerable amounts.

The biggest areas to test are:

First, your front cover headline, and product headlines. If you have one product or service, test a number of different cover headlines, and sub-headlines in your product copy.

If you have a multi-product brochure test each different product headline and track sales results. Every square inch in your brochure should justify itself in profitable sales. If any product doesn't sell well even after testing different, more compelling headlines, dump it and replace it with another product, and start testing again. This process will soon lead you to discover the highest selling products and headlines.

Second, test different copy. One appeal can outsell another by multiples. If you fail to test different appeals, you'll never know how much more you can garner from the same brochure.

Third, test prices. One price can out-sell a different price by three times or more.

Fourth, test your ordering device. Make sure it is easy to understand. Make sure you 'lead customers by the hand' through the ordering process. (See Chapter 18 for details on testing.)

Next — **7 Rapid Business Multipliers: How To Generate £10,000 - £100,000 New Business And Cash, Virtually Overnight...**

PART 4

7 Rapid Business Multipliers — How To Generate £10,000 - £100,000 New Business And Cash, Virtually Overnight

CHAPTER 18

Rapid Business Multiplier #1:
Test, And Market The
Clear Winner

Have you ever been given a birthday gift you really didn't want? Usually a piece of clothing or perfume or aftershave that just isn't your style? You thank your benefactor but you silently think *if only he asked what I would like!*

Does it surprise you that most businesses make the same mistake when selling their products—and lose countless sales as a result?

Most businesses—and disarmingly, also advertising agencies—put sales messages out and assume **they** know which sales appeal out of many, customers will respond to in greatest numbers. Heads of business and agency copywriters think that what appeals to **them** will also appeal to the masses. Ninety-nine times out of one hundred they are wrong.

Consequently, innumerable sales are unknowingly lost with every campaign.

The one... *and only...* way to ensure your sales message appeals to the greatest number of prospective customers is to **'ask'** them personally.

Go To The Court of Last Resort

The **buyers** of your product or service are the **only** people who have the right, and the ability, to judge which sales appeal they prefer. They are the court of last resort.

Go to them with a small, low-cost sales test plus a method of tracking response, and they will soon tell you whether they like it or not, **by the number of their orders.**

If you do not test every element of marketing you do, and you do not accurately track every response, you are without question losing thousands, hundreds of thousands, or millions of pounds of additional sales and multiplied profits that **you could be making for the same effort, and for the same cost.**

Testing: The Scientific key To Optimizing Your Response

You can increase your sales geometrically by up to *hundreds of percent* by simply first running small, low cost tests on all your marketing, then rolling it out with the appeal which proved itself to be a clear winner. How? **You test specific elements of your marketing against similar elements to find the combination that prospective customers respond to most.**

When you do test, you'll discover that one headline or opening statement will out-sell another by up to 2,100 times. One sales 'story' will sell more product than another by two, three, four times, or more. One price will appeal to customers significantly more than a lower — or **higher** — price. One bonus offer can prove more popular by 50%, 100%, 300%. One guarantee can win buyers trust more than a lessor guarantee, and increase your sales by up to three hundred percent.

A Stark Example

A few months ago I asked a large room of seminar attendees this question: if you were a vacuum cleaner manufacturer, and you ran adverts in the national press with the headline:

Clean Every Room In Your House <u>More Easily</u> With The New Easyglide, Light Weight Bugsucker

...how do you know that 'more easily' and 'light weight' is

what the majority of vacuum cleaner buyers want? Of course, you and I don't know. At this stage we are just guessing.

The fast way to find out, and to multiply your sales quickly, is to test different appeals. For instance, you could test the headline above against the alternative headline:

Suck-up More Dust, Dirt, Mites and Bugs With The Amazing Bugsucker... The Most Powerful Vacuum on Earth

Both headlines are good. But which one will appeal more to vacuum cleaner buyers? Will there be a large discrepancy or will customers respond to both appeals equally?

Let's find out.

I asked everyone who prefers headline one to raise their hand. Hands went up. Then I asked everyone who prefers headline two to raise their hands. A different number of hands were raised.

What do *you* think? Did you guess correctly? The answer is: headline two was the winner. But here's the surprise—headline two out-pulled headline one by a significant 3 to 1. One quarter of the room preferred headline one; *three quarters responded to headline two.*

If you had blindly opted for headline one because *you* thought it powerful, you would miss out on three hundred percent more sales *at no extra cost.*

(NOTE: I tested these headlines for seminar attendees as a demonstration only. When **you** test, you should do so with actual sales offers. See the *TIP* on page 178.)

Two of The Worst Offending Institutions

Banks and investment companies are two of the worst examples of untested, institutional advertising and marketing. The handful that do test run away with the biggest volume of business.

One investment company ran half page ads in the national press with the headline:

THE MOST IMPORTANT INVESTMENT DECISION OF YOUR LIFE

Someone, somewhere (probably their advertising agency), in their wisdom, obviously took it upon their shoulders to decide that **this headline appeal** would be most appealing to prospective customers.

It might be. Although I doubt it. It doesn't tell you anything about the benefits you will derive by investing with the company, or what advantages you will gain by choosing them rather than a competitor.

But it's easy to find the answer!; go to the court of last appeal — in this case the investing public. I would bet that a different headline would produce more response, perhaps by two or three times, or more. Here's one:

Over the last 5 years, 112,814 ordinary people made an average 19.2% <u>each</u> <u>year</u> on money invested with (name of company).

You can now join them. Invest as little as £1,000 — or £50 a month — and you can become a winning investor too.

or,

Why put your money into a low-interest high street account when the <u>same money</u> can make you over 19% a year? That's what 112,814 small investors made every year, over the last 5 years.

Here's a free investment report that reveals how easy it is for you to become a winning investor too.

This company is spending £35,000 on each advert. If it is making a profit on the existing ads, it can easily multiply its profits two, three, four, or more times *simply by testing different headlines* and choosing the clear winner.

Such is the power of testing.

Test Safe and Small, Then Roll-Out The Winner With No Risk

Test various different appeals in a small way, to 100, 1,000, or 5,000 (maximum) prospects. The **one sales appeal** that most customers respond to **by purchasing** is the winning test. Customers are saying: *We prefer **this** sales appeal! More of us will buy more of your product when you present it in **this** manner!*

When you have tested on a small basis and found the winning combination, you can be reasonably sure your response will remain the same when you market to a bigger audience. Human nature is human nature. Roll out your winning test to a larger test audience of say two or three times the size, and track response. Then expand your test to two or three times the size of your *second* test and so on.

TIP:
Running **actual sales tests** is the only scientific way to discover what your prospective customers will respond to. Fortunes have been lost with market research that asks hypothetical customers what they will respond to *if they received this letter, or product promotion, or sample*. What people *say* they will do and what they will *actually* do when they have to part with money are often completely different.

The only sure way to discover what people *will* buy is to ask them to buy it now.

Split-Run Tests Give The Fast Answer

If you are test mailing 5,000 prospective customers, split them into say, three groups of 1,666. Mail each 1,666 with a different version of the same offer. Send either three different letters, or state a different price, or provide a different guarantee, or ask for a different call to action.

If you want to test different adverts, run say, two different ads simultaneously in two different regions of a newspaper or magazine. (Papers and magazines often print different issues for different areas of the country. The least that some UK media print is *two editions* — one north, one south.) If the publication you want to advertise in prints only one blanket edition, the next best test is to run two, three, or four different ads (each with their own 'code') one after the other.

Track the response you get from each of the mailing groups, or test ads. You will soon have the answers telling you which headline, letter, offer, price, guarantee, or call to action pulls most response.

5 Elements You Should Test First

Every element of your offer can make a difference to your response, right down to the colour of paper you use, the envelope you mail your offer in, and the month and week in which you make your offer. But the elements that create the *biggest* difference in response, and that you should test first, are:

1.   **Headline or opening statement of ad, letter, or brochure.**

2.   **Selling copy of offer itself — the body copy.**

Remember, the **only** thing your customer wants to know about your product or service is, ***"What's in it for me?"*** Make sure all your marketing is written and designed with your <u>customer or client</u> in mind, not you.

3.   **Guarantee/risk-reversal.**

4.   **Price.**

I have seen £29.95 out pull £31.95 two to one, and £69 outsell £71 by three times. I've also seen £99 sell twice as many products as £49. And most amazingly, I've seen £15,000 sell almost as much as £3,500. Guess which was more profitable!

The price is only right when prospective customers *perceive* it to be right. The 'right' price is usually the one *most customers respond to*. (Sometimes your aim might be to acquire *quality* customers, not volume. In this case, you may want to charge a higher price to ensure you only attract serious buyers. Or you may find you make higher up-front profits by selling less, but at a higher price, if up-front profits are your best long-term strategy. High fulfilment costs might be such that less volume, but higher-value sales will give you more profit.)

5.   Call to action.

Always tell your readers, listeners or viewers *specifically* what action you want them to take next. For instance, if you want customers to phone or send for more information, tell them specifically what to do. You could say,

"Find out why the Bugsucker will keep your house cleaner than ever before. Phone freephone 0800 BUGSUCKER now for a free copy of the special consumer report, **How To Banish Dust, Dirt, Mites & Bugs from your house forever with the powerful new Bugsucker Vacuum** plus details of the <u>free</u> settee and curtain vacuum you'll receive with Bugsucker, worth £72"

If you want customers to order directly, tell them specifically how to order. You could say,

"To order, simply **phone 0800 BUGSUCKER now** and tell our sales assistant you'd like to order the new Bugsucker Vacuum. Have your credit card, name and address and telephone number ready, so that we can dispatch your order immediately.

Or if you prefer, complete the order form below, and send it to us now in the freepost envelope provided. Your Bugsucker Vacuum will be dispatched to you by return."

7.   The ordering device.

A complicated ordering process can reduce your response dramatically. Test different ordering devices. Make it *easy* for your customers to respond by simplifying the process of buying whatever it is you are selling.

Call-to-Action Elements To Test

Adverts/Flyers/Inserts: If you are asking for response from adverts, flyers, or inserts including a reply coupon will generally increase response. Ask customers to fill-in the coupon and return it to your address now. Or ask them to call you right away to place their order.

Letters: At the end of your letter provide clear, simple, logical instructions on how you want your reader to respond. The rule of thumb is: the more easy-to-understand, straightforward, and logical your call to action is, the higher response you'll achieve.

Brochures: If you send a brochure and other information, always provide an easy-to-follow order form, logically laid out, with your address, plus a fax and telephone number if they want to order by fax or phone. It is usually beneficial to include a free-post or reply-paid envelope.

TV or Radio: If you advertise on TV or radio, always tell people what action to take next. Make it simple; prospects have only *seconds* to remember or jot down what they should do to respond. Give people an *easy* address and/or telephone number to remember. Try to get a memorable freephone number, or vanity number like 0800 NEWCAR, 0800 OFFICECLEAN, 0800 COMPUTER, 0800 PINESHOP, for example.

TIP:

A freephone number can increase your response by up to 30 percent. I advise nearly all my clients to get one. Why go to all the effort and expense of producing an effective marketing campaign only to lose up to 30 percent of the sales by asking customers to pay for their call? Although it's only a small cost to them, it's a quirk of human nature that stops some customers calling if they are asked to pay.

TIP:

Vanity numbers can increase sales because they are easy to re-member. British Telecom usually issues freephone 0800 numbers with a maximum of 6 or 7 digits. But you can have more letters than numbers in your vanity name, if you wish. For instance, if you wanted 0800 PINESHOP, BT would probably issue you with a 7-digit number which would be: 0800 7463746—which spells 0800 PINESHO on your telephone key pad. You can add the 'P' to com-plete your vanity number *without affecting incoming calls.* BT's ex-change ignores the added number (in this case the added number '7' for 'P'.)

TIP:

The same applies to your address—you generally receive more response with a freepost address, or reply-paid envelope. Not always though. Test it. One point: freepost is delivered by *second class* mail. So your customers have to wait at least one extra day for you to receive their request, or order. I personally like to use a freepost address in adverts only (for those who prefer to write rather than phone), so customers can write immediately with-out having to buy a stamp. Every other form of marketing can have a first class reply-paid facility **printed** on it.

How To Draw Customers Into Retail Stores In Droves

If you are advertising to increase sales of your product in stores, always provide people with a **reason to respond now.** Test dif-ferent response *reasons.* To get customers to visit a store to try or buy your product you must motivate them with a powerful call to action.

Make it easy and tempting! Have an introductory offer, or a free prize draw, or a bonus product (2 for 1 works well), or a collection points scheme, or an affiliation with another product they can buy with a price advantage, or a coupon promotion at-tached to your product. There are dozens of other possibilities.

The important point is: **always, always** leave your customer with strong motivation and simple instructions on what next step he or she should take to sample or buy your product or service, or to obtain more information.

How To Test And Find Your Biggest Winning Formula

If you test more than one element at a time you will not know which is making the difference to response.

Let's assume you have created a mail package you are happy with—consisting of a letter, a colour brochure, an order form, and a reply-paid envelope. You are going to test it with a mailing to 5,000 prospective customers.

Send your original package to one-third of the list—1,666. Now take one element of your package, write two different versions of it, and send those to the other two lots of 1,666.

I would first test **two different headlines or opening statements** on my *letter*. Keep the body copy of the letter the same; just test two different headlines, so you have three headlines altogether.

You'll discover one of your headlines out-pulls the other two, maybe by a large margin.

That headline becomes your 'control'—the one you will keep. Now test three different *prices*. Again you'll find one price proves more popular than the two other prices. Use *that* price as your control in all your next tests.

Keep testing each major element in your mailing until you finish up with the largest responding combination. Ninety times out of a hundred you will find you generate as much as *hundreds of percent more sales* with the winning combination of tested elements than you were with your original piece.

Apply the same procedure to every element of your marketing to find the winning appeal from adverts, letters, brochures, flyers, inserts, blow-ins, telemarketing, point-of-sale, price tags, window promotions, cross-sales, up-sales, guarantees, the approach your salespeople make and so on.

Testing is indeed a rapid business multiplier.

CHAPTER 19

Rapid Business Multiplier #2: Communicate Regularly With Your Customers or Clients

Your most certain and profitable growth will come from your **existing customers** or clients. Surprisingly, even if you sell a 'one-shot' product like property, replacement windows, wedding gowns, domestic appliances and so on, your existing customers are the source of your biggest growth in profits.

The profit-generating potential of existing customers is a much misunderstood and unrealised opportunity in business. Your **customers** are the single most valuable asset you have as a business owner.

Let me repeat that so it burns itself into your mind:

*Your customers or clients are the single
most valuable asset you have*

Acquiring a new customer is the most expensive thing a business ever does. Yet most businesses pour money and their largest sales efforts into acquiring new customers and then fail to nurture the relationship as the customer would like. This is a big mistake.

Acquiring New Customers is Your Single Biggest Cost

Winning new customers is your most expensive task. On average, it costs you *nine times more* to acquire a new customer as it does to sell to an existing customer.

Before a prospect will favour you with a purchase you have to capture her attention, cultivate interest, demonstrate your unique advantage, gain her confidence, and earn her trust. This costs time, effort and money. You have to advertise, mail expensive sales materials, dispatch expensive salespeople, follow up. You have to nurture your prospect until she is ready to buy.

When she *does* buy, you have overcome the natural barrier between prospective buyer, and seller. Your new customer has said *Yes, I am willing to become part of your buying family because I like you and trust you.*

At this stage you have gained a new asset of almost incalculable value. Why? Because — *as long as you nurture your customer respectfully, intelligently, regularly, and with favour* — he or she will be the source of a snowballing sales influx. Better still, the cost of generating future sales from existing customers is **tiny** compared with acquiring those customers in the first place.

Every Customer is a Ready Source of Additional Sales

As long as you never do anything to abuse their trust, and you regularly nurture the seller/buyer relationship, every customer is a ready source of additional sales.

A customer acquired ethically and honestly will trust your selling advice again, and repeatedly. If you ask him to recommend you to his family, friends, colleagues, social associates, **he will** because you already added value in some way to his life.

How To Communicate With Your Customers

Write or telephone your customers regularly with news of updates to your product lines, extended services, preferential prices, package offers, special one-offs, add-ons, extras, new releases, limited stocks, favoured service. Keep them in touch with every benefit and advantage that will add value to their purchase and be a source of additional income for you. Show your customers you care about them. Make people feel special as part of your customer family.

But wait. People get fed-up with a continual barrage of sales letters and telephone calls, right? Wrong — with one caveat.

If you make the mistake of disrespecting your customers with empty sales hype you will quickly lose their attention.

But if you respect and treat your customers *as you like to be treated* by communicating genuine value, benefit, advantage they will listen to you, respect you, and be willing to take your advice.

The Secret Of Successful Customer Communication

If you feed your customers or clients with interesting, informative, educational, and newsworthy information, *you cannot communicate too much.*

Never send blatant sales-hype. **It doesn't work.** Instead, send an interesting, thoughtful and respectful offer.

Communicate to your *customers* exactly as you would to your *best friend.*

Think about it. If your closest friend showed interest in buying your spare car, you wouldn't start blabbing off a barrage of empty sales hype, would you?

You would be honest. You would take care to explain every detail. You would point out the particular features you think would benefit him most. You would present both sides of the story — the good and the *not* so good.

Finally you would let your friend know the price he can buy it for, and how to pay you. You would even deliver it for him if it helped. You may even say to him, take it and try it for a month. If you don't like it after that simply bring it back. I don't want you to have it if it isn't going to suit you a hundred percent.

This is what the smartest, and wealthiest, sellers do. They are honest, ethical, interested in their *customer's satisfaction* even before their own, and in nurturing their customer long-term.

But for some reason, marketing and sales people think they have to be different when it comes to selling to *customers*. They assume it is a different process. So they sit and produce reams of

186

pure sales hype, marketing slight of hand, institutional glitz that does not *inform,* and 'creative' advertising that does not *sell*.

Why? Why is selling to your customer fundamentally any different than selling to your closest friend? It isn't! People see through sales hype. They do not trust it. And they largely **do not respond to it.**

3 Golden Rules to Increase Customer Response

1. People dislike being **sold** to.
   They like receiving **advice** on how to make the wisest buying decision.

2. People dislike being **told.**
   They like being **guided.**

3. People dislike being **part of the crowd.**
   They like being recognised as **individuals.**

Incorporate these three golden rules into all your communication with customers, and they will respond with willing cheque books.

Communicate Intelligently, Sincerely And Honestly

Consider these statistical facts. When you make a 'cold' marketing effort to prospective customers—usually a direct mail pack, a flyer, or a telemarketing campaign—you will achieve between nought and 1% response. (I have seen as high as 3% but it's rare and usually only possible to highly targeted prospects.) You should calculate your offer on 0.5% response. If it goes better, great! But don't bet your money on receiving a higher return.

But when you make an offer to your **existing customers** you will achieve a response up to 5%, 7%, 10%, 17%, or higher. These are all real returns I have received by communicating with customers.

In other words, you can garner **10 times** to **34 times** more response *for no extra expenditure of money or time,* than you can

187

marketing cold. More graphically, if you make regular, interesting offers to your existing customer base, you can make **1,000% to 3,400% more sales** than if you made the **same offer** to *prospective* customers. It's a massive leveraging opportunity.

Communicate regularly with your existing customers intelligently, sincerely, and honestly. Inform them, interest them, educate them on your product or service range.

I haven't Got My Customers Names! What Do I do?

If you sell to the public, start capturing your customers names and addresses and write to them *at least* monthly.

How? Run a prize draw. Get your printer to design small entry slips on which customers can write their name, address, and telephone. Also include a birthday and 'special-dates' line. Some customers will not feel comfortable giving this information but most will. You then have another *reason* to write, with a congratulatory message and a special occasion offer.

TIP:
Make your prize big enough to interest nearly every customer. A small retailer can offer a top prize of £50 and ten or twenty runner-up prizes of £10 each. Or you can give twice the value at no more cost. How? Give vouchers redeemable against stock. Every voucher redeemed at retail value costs only the trade price of the stock, often 50 percent of the retail price.

A national business can give away more but it is often not necessary.

If you are manufacturing and/or selling to trade and business buyers, you almost certainly record customer details on each invoice.

Start *using* your customer database to communicate regularly along the lines I have explained. Always remember your customer database is the most valuable asset you possess. If you treat every customer with the utmost respect *you cannot communicate too often.*

Communicating Increases Sales—Even If You Sell A One-Shot Product!

You sell a one-shot product. Property, replacement windows, wedding gowns, domestic appliances, pets, property extensions, stone driveways. Surely these and other one-time product customers cannot be the source of extra sales, right?

Wrong.

Let me ask you this. If you buy a house, does it mean you'll never buy another house?

Does it mean you don't know any *other people* who will want to buy a house? Family, friends, relatives, colleagues, social associates?

Of course you do! You are likely to know dozens of people, many of whom you are in contact with regularly.

Now let me ask you this. If I was the Estate Agent you bought your house from, and one week after you'd moved in I contacted you to ask if everything was alright, and if you were happy, and if there was anything else I could do or advise you on that would help you, would you be surprised that I had taken the trouble to call? I think you probably would be.

Wouid you tell your friends and work colleagues how good your Estate Agent was to call and check if everything was OK? Yes, you almost certainly would.

What if, after one month, I wrote to you with a useful piece of information on keeping draughts out and reducing your heating bill? Would you value that information? You bet.

What if **every** month I sent you helpful and informative information on how to improve your home—decorating tips, a great curtain supplier one of my other clients told me about, a carpet dealer who sells top brands at lower prices, gardening tips, a quick note highlighting a new TV programme about loft conversions, and so on.

Would this be valuable and interesting to you? Maybe not all of it. **But much of what I sent probably would interest most home owners.** Either way, you would almost certainly appreciate the effort I take to help you and inform you, *especially as I am receiving no apparent gain.*

Would you tell your friends and colleagues how *great* your Estate Agent was for being so helpful and valuing you as a client? You almost certainly would!

Now, when any of your family, friends, colleagues, or social associates move house, who do you think they will want to buy from? Me! Why? Because you recommended me. Because I demonstrated that I *care*. That I value every person who buys from me. That I take the trouble to *keep in touch after the sale* and be a catalyst of additional, useful information and assistance.

Wedding Gown Store Grows 40% in 12 Months

The owner of a successful wedding gown store wanted to know how to increase her sales further. She already marketed with effective advertising, a good range of gowns, competitive prices, and a first class service. What else could she do?

She was advised to start communicating with her customers. To write to them *after they bought a gown,* thanking them and offering best wishes for their big day. To write *after the wedding* with an invitation to attend a post-wedding champagne celebration at the store. To write on anniversaries and birthdays. Also, to write to them every month with details of the latest wedding gown styles in stock.

Within 12 months this store owner had increased her sales by over 40 percent. Just by keeping in touch. How? *Because every bride nearly always knows other brides-to-be.* By showing *her* brides that she cared, she quickly built a team of enthusiastic ambassadors who said to every newly engaged friend *you must buy your gown from this store!*

Your largest and fastest and most profitable growth will come from the one source you don't have to spend extra cash converting — your existing customers. Always communicate regularly with them.

190

CHAPTER 20

Rapid Business Multiplier #3: Start a Profit-Generating Database

If, somehow, you could **accurately predict** what your customers wanted to buy every month think of the extra sales you could make! What would they be worth in your case — £1,000? £5,000? £10,000? £100,000? £1,000,000? predicting and understanding your customers buying habits is worth big money.

But surely predicting the future buying desires of your customers is impossible, right? Wrong! Modern technology has not only made it possible but *affordable,* even for the tiny one-person business.

The Mighty Sales Power of Database Marketing

Tracking the personal details and buying habits of your customers on a computer database arms you with three powerful competitive advantages.

1. You can regularly *communicate* with your customers in a personalised, meaningful manner that they respond to.

2. You can accurately *predict* customers future buying preferences and target your sales messages accordingly.

3.   You can organise high-profit joint-venture and host/recipient alliances to targeted groups of customers.

In the days before personal computers keeping a database was time-consuming and expensive. Companies who knew the sales-multiplying effect of good communication maintained thousands of handwritten or typed index cards with customer profiles and buying histories.

Now, you can keep these 'index cards' on your PC database, target selected customers at the push of a key, and merge their names, addresses and other individual buying information into personalised mailings in minutes.

Biggest Profits Are Attainable Only By *Targeting* Customers

If you send sales messages out to a blanket market you can never optimize response. Why? Because customers *tend* to buy within the same quality sphere, price range, and area of interest they have bought in before.

If you own a high quality shoe store with exclusive ranges from the finest Italian shoe makers, there is little sales potential in marketing to people who tend to only buy *inexpensive* shoes.

On the other hand, if you sell shoes at competitive prices, and you appeal to a volume market, there is little sales potential in marketing to buyers of exclusive Italian shoes.

Likewise, if you sell a wide range of products, there is little sales potential in marketing cold-weather hiking coats to customers who have only bought *dress shoes* from you. Why? Because they have never shown any interest in cold-weather hiking coats. Just dress shoes.

To garner more profits from your existing customers market the same *type* and *quality* of product or service as they have proven they are interested in by their past purchasing.

Market exclusive Italian shoes to exclusive Italian shoe buyers, inexpensive volume-market shoes to inexpensive shoe buyers, cold-weather hiking coats to cold-weather hikers.

How To Engineer 2 - 4 Times More Sales From Every Marketing Pound

If you own a shoe store and stock a good selection of styles and price ranges to attract a wide market, some of your customers will always tend to buy *expensive* shoes, others *mid-priced* shoes, and others *low-priced* shoes.

Let's say 20 percent of customers buy your expensive range, 60 percent your mid-range, 20 percent your low range. Knowing this, you have a secret weapon with which to market.

When a new range of mid-priced shoes became available, if you marketed them to your whole customer database, the twenty percent of high-priced shoe buyers, and the twenty percent of low-priced shoe buyers will probably not be interested in your mailing. Two things will happen.

1. They will throw it away.

2. They will remember your mailing does not apply to *them*. Next time you mail them they will not pay you the attention they would if they knew all your mailings *did* apply to them.

If, on the other hand, you sent a promotional introduction about your newest mid-priced range to only those sixty percent of customers who buy mid-priced shoes, *you would be talking directly to the most likely buyers*.

Remember:

The more you target the historical buying habits and desires of your customers, the more profits you make

Conversely, the *less* you target your customers the more marketing pounds you throw away.

An added bonus of database marketing is that you can market highly effectively without your competitors discovering what you're doing. Unlike advertising, database marketing is invisible to competitors. Only your customers get to see your offers, what headline appeals you are using, what persuasive body copy you have written, what guarantees and prices you are offering. All this 'underground' marketing gives you a powerful head start against tough competitors who want to sell to the same market.

Make Offers Based On Customers Buying History

If you mailed a blanket sales promotion to your database, and you received a 5 percent response, you would probably make a good profit.

But if you *targeted* your customers and mailed them offers *based on their previous buying habits* you could increase your response to 7%, 10%, 12%, 17%, or higher. All these are actual responses received by targeted database marketing.

Your sales can double, or more. But your profits multiply by three, four, five or more times because the **cost of your campaign is the same** whether you receive a low response, or a high response.

Business Owners Increase Sales 40 - 60 Percent

In my experience, when you start a targeted and systematic database marketing campaign you will increase your sales by between 40 to 60 percent within twelve months *almost without fail.*

With fast, low cost PC's, powerful database software, and high quality printers available on almost every street corner today, all businesses can now take advantage of the additional sales and profits a database campaign can generate.

If you own a small business and you don't already own a modern PC, I urge you to buy one. The extra profits you will earn from target marketing will quickly recoup your investment and aid you in dramatic new growth. £2,000 to £3,000 will buy you the PC, printer and database software you need.

If you already own a PC, printer and database software and you're not using it to mail regular targeted database promotions, you can grow your sales significantly, almost overnight, without any further equipment investment.

TIP:

If you don't want to splash out for new equipment, consider buying second-hand. There are a number of good dealers around the country who'll help you with reliable used equipment. Make sure you get a good warranty. It's usually best to find a dealer near you in case anything develops a fault. Many suppliers also provide fairly low-cost yearly maintenance contracts. These range from about £50 to £130 per PC depending on the company. A service engineer will then come to you and repair the fault.

I have found a company in London to be very good. They are: **Morgan Computer Company,** 64 New Oxford Street, London WC1A. Telephone 0171 255 2115.

TIP:

The database software you choose will include instructions on what type of PC is required to run it. You'll probably—at a minimum—need a 200 MHz processor, 8 MB of RAM, at least 30 MB of available space on your hard drive, and Microsoft Windows 95 or 98, but check the software instructions and ask your dealer for advice.

A laser printer is more versatile and produces better quality text and images than dot matrix or bubble jet printers. A 300 or 600dpi laser printer is perfectly sufficient and nowadays very affordable. What cost £600-£1,000 two years ago costs £300-£500 now.

A system like the above is ideal for most small businesses. If you run a bigger business, or you need more elaborate information from your database—to keep track of every item sold in a retail store linked to particular customers, or if you send hundreds of thousands of personalised mailings each month—you can buy more sophisticated networked systems for £10,000+ that make light of the job.

The point is: Database marketing—whether you run a tiny, medium, or huge business—offers you substantial additional sales opportunities. It is worth investing in a system that will handle your business effectively and with ease.

10 Records You Need To Start a Successful Database

Start capturing the names, addresses, telephone numbers and other relevant details of your customers. Also record every product or type of service they buy from you.

Your aim is to build-up an accurate *buying history* of every customer. This historical information forms the foundational core of your database campaign.

Here are the 10 records you need to start a successful database:

1. Name of individual.

2. Name of company/organisation.

3. Full mailing address, including post code.

4. Telephone number and, if business customers, fax number and e-mail address.

5. Source of inquiry or order, i.e. advert, catalogue, telephone, sales person contact, retail store, etc.

6. Date and/or purchase details of first inquiry or order.

7. Recency/frequency/monetary purchase history, i.e.:
    A) Date
    B) Cumulative amount of purchases in pounds
    C) Product, or product lines purchased (or services.)

8. Credit history with you and credit rating system (a scoring system works well.)

9. Relevant demographic information for individual buyers: age, gender, marital status, family data, education, income, occupation.

10. For industrial buyers: type of company, size of company, revenues, number of employees.

5 Secrets To High-Profit Database Marketing

1. **Target your sales messages according to your customers buying history.**

Send top of the range offers to top of the range buyers. Mid-range offers to mid-range buyers. Low-range offers to low-range buyers.

2. **Communicate *more* with your best customers.**

If you discover 20 percent of your customers **spend more** than others, communicate with this special group more often. The more a customer spends with you, the more they usually **will** spend with you in future — if you market to them intelligently, respectfully, and interestingly.

Also, if you discover a percentage of customers buy more **frequently** than others, communicate with *this* group more, too.

Offer your preferential customers preferential treatment! You can offer them first choice on new stock or new services, upgrade options, preferential add-on sales, additional bonuses, special discounts, cross-buying opportunities, etc. You can invite them to pre-sale viewings, product or service launches, special events.

The more you make your customers feel *special* and *respected* the more they will respond by purchasing.

3. **Send your customers birthday, Christmas, Easter and special occasion gifts, offers, and 'personalised' buying opportunities.**

4. ***After*** **the sale, send your customers additional, helpful information, instructions, or education that will add value to their purchase in some way, or their *use* of what they purchased.**

5.   **Communicate with your customers regularly, with updates of your latest products and services and an opportunity to buy.**

You Cannot Communicate Too Much

Can you communicate too much? No! You can only communicate too *boringly* or with too much *sales-hype*. As long as you speak to your customers in an interesting, respectful, educational, informative, helpful, intelligent manner *you cannot communicate too much.*

Targeted database marketing provides you with powerful competitive advantage in an age when competition is fierce. Knowing who your best customers are, what they buy, and how often they buy provides you with an effective marketing weapon.

The more you communicate, and the more effectively you do so, **the more you sell** without your competitors discovering how you are achieving it.

CHAPTER 21

Rapid Business Multiplier #4: Discover What Your Customers and Prospects *Really Want* and Give it to Them

I am puzzled why more business owners never take the time to determine exactly what their existing customers **really want.**

In the majority of cases, once a prospect becomes a customer by making their first purchase, he or she is favourably disposed toward buying **more** from you in the future. If you consistently provide what customers want the majority will continue buying from you for years or even decades.

What better way to find out what your customers want, and often *need,* than to simply **ask them?**

Travel Agent's Sales Boom

A man in the travel agency business came to me. He was finding it difficult making his fledgling enterprise more profitable.

But this entrepreneur was unknowingly harbouring a valuable asset he could cash-in on almost instantly—his customers!

Selling travel has become extremely competitive. And because the cost of supplying airline travel and hotel accommodation constitutes a high proportion of the ticket price, travel agents margins are low, typically ten percent. To make money you have to sell volume.

By the time he'd paid his advertising, overhead, and staff, he was left with only a tiny profit at the end of the month.

But he owned over three thousand valuable assets — **customers** — that had booked holidays with him in the past. Like most businesses though, he never thought to **ask** these customers what their future travel preferences were. He did business in the reverse way. He advertised, and displayed in his three shops, holidays **he** decided would be of interest to customers.

In effect he was saying, "These are the holidays we offer, come in and give us money for them." It was a *me* message. Most travel agents, *and other businesses,* market themselves in the same way. But it is a big mistake. A 'me' message will always limit the amount of sales you can achieve.

I suggested he prepare and mail a comprehensive, interesting, and tantalizing *questionnaire* to every one of his 3,000+ customers, asking what their travel preferences were for the coming year. *Where* in the world would they like to visit? What *type* of holiday interests them — relaxing beaches? Adventurous treks? Historical sights? Hiking? Canoeing? Ocean cruising? What time of year do they like to take their holiday? What restaurants, night life, child facilities, car hire do they prefer? Altogether, we asked over one hundred pertinent questions.

How did customers respond? In droves. They appreciated the fact this travel agent **cared enough about them to ask** what they would like him to offer.

Instead of *his* travel agent, it became *theirs.* They could custom-order any holiday they wanted.

Ironically, almost all travel agents can custom-make practically any type of holiday. But because this agent *asked,* his customers were predisposed towards *him.*

Did the questionnaire increase his sales? What do you think! There on his desk were hundreds of people saying, "Please give me the opportunity to buy **this** type of holiday from you!" What more can you ever want from your customers?

He now possesses the information he needs to market **targeted holiday offers** direct to each holiday category on his database. Customers that have asked for relaxing tropical beach holidays are sent information on relaxing tropical beach holidays. Customers that have asked for skiing holidays are sent information on skiing holidays. And so on through every category.

He now knows that every pound spent on mailing promotional material is optimized because it is received by people who have asked for holiday details in that category.

Already, four months short of a full year's marketing, he's nearly **doubled his sales** this year. And profits are high because he is generating the additional sales from the same three shops, the same number of staff, and almost the same marketing investment. He just leveraged the assets he already had.

How To Ask *Your* Customers What They Really Want

You can ask your customers what they want by:

1. Sending them an interesting and comprehensive questionnaire.

2. Asking them, "What has to happen to make this purchase perfect for you?"

3. Asking them, "What else (or what other range) would you like us to stock that you may be interested in buying?"

4. Asking them, "How can we improve our products/ service/staff/premises to make buying from us an even better experience?"

Make it a priority to ask your customers and prospects what they really want from you. Then take action on what they tell you by *making it available to them.*

A wise man once said, "You have two ears, and only one mouth, **for a reason.**" One of the most valuable habits any business person can develop is *asking the right questions*, listening intensely to the answers, then taking action to provide resultant solutions.

I believe the art of *listening* is worth one thousand times more than the indulgence of talking. Especially in business.

CHAPTER 22

Rapid Business Multiplier #5: Make it *Easy* and *Pleasureable* For Customers To Buy From You

How many times have you walked into a store, eaten at a restaurant, requested a brochure, ordered a product by mail... only to find yourself *frustrated* by the poor service you received?

I doubt it is only me who constantly gets frustrated with service that is not *customer-oriented*. In short, if you don't make my whole buying experience with you efficient, easy, pleasurable I will not be endeared to buy from you.

We all know a number of businesses that are booming. A busy restaurant. A great store. A car dealership that sells two or three times more cars than its competitors. What baffles me is that right there, for any business owner to pick-up ideas from, are blueprints for success. Yet most entrepreneurs, directors, and professionals never seem to put two and two together. They never put themselves in their customer's shoes and realise that by improving their service they would massively increase their sales.

See Your Business From Your Customer's Point of View

If you want to optimize your selling potential to each customer you have to regularly *look at your business from your customer's point of view*, by:

1. Buying your own product.

2. Requesting your own information.

3. Visiting your own premises.

4. Speaking to your own staff.

5. Experiencing your own service.

With competitors vying for your customers, it's more important than ever to provide a second-to-none service. The more you make buying from you easy, efficient, and pleasurable the more customers **will** buy from you.

A 33-Point Check-Up For Your Business

Note: Not every one of these points will apply to your business, but most probably **will**. Tick as many points as you think **do** or **could** apply to your business. Then check your commitment to each point at least every week, and ideally every *day*.

1. Is your store/premises spotlessly clean?
2. Are your carpets vacuumed and clean?
3. Is it freshly painted inside and out?
4. Is the pavement washed and swept?
5. Are your fittings or shelves scratch-free and dusted clean?
6. Is the temperature invitingly warm in winter and refreshingly cool in summer?
7. Does your store/showroom smell attractive?
8. Are your goods displayed attractively and in an easy-to-find manner?
9. Does every item you sell have a price tag? Is the price tag attractive?
10. Do the fittings, lighting, and decoration reflect the quality and pricing of your store/showroom/premises?

11. Are your staff helpful, knowledgeable, and interested?
12. Do your staff **always** put the customer before *anything* else?
13. Do you stock **enough quantity** to ensure a customer never has to walk out without what he or she wants?
14. Can you get out-of-stock items **fast** for a customer who wants to order? In two days? One day? A few hours? Within one hour?
15. Can the staff member who answers the phone give knowledgable, helpful and authoritative advice?
16. Can you guarantee to never keep a customer waiting on the phone while someone who **can** answer the questions is found?
17. Do **all** your staff **always** greet **every** customer with a genuine smile whether it is face-to-face, or on the telephone?
18. Do all your staff show genuine, helpful interest to every customer?
19. Do all your staff greet every customer with good eye contact?
20. Do all your staff listen intently to your customer's needs?
21. Do all your staff offer a genuine serving attitude?
22. Do you respond to every request immediately by sending information out the **same day by first class mail?**
23. Is your reception area clean, organised, professional, and impressive?
24. Are your chairs comfortable?
25. Are your tables solid? (Wobbly tables are so annoying!)
26. Is your cutlery and glassware spotless?
27. Are your table cloths spotless and ironed?
28. Are your staff dressed appropriately? (Do they have a uniform, a colour coordination? Do they 'look' like professional staff who belong to your professional business?)

29. Do your staff thoroughly and authoritatively know about what they are selling? Have they used it, experienced it, eaten it, worn it, travelled in it?
30. Is your food as hot, or as cold as it should be?
31. Do you serve *enough* food?
32. Do you, and your staff, go the extra mile to please, help, and even *astonish* your customers?

and finally...

33. Are your customer and staff toilets always kept *as clean, fresh, and comfortable* as you keep yours at home?

Become a customer of yours for the day. See what *they* see. Experience what *they* experience when inquiring, ordering, and buying your products or services.

(Or, because your staff will be on best behaviour with **you** present, send in an anonymous inspector.)

Start a suggestions box where customers and *staff* can suggest ideas to improve the quality of what you sell, the supremacy of the service you provide, and the attractiveness and functionality of your premises.

Send your customers a questionnaire asking them what they would like to see your business do to make buying from you more appropriate, efficient, enjoyable. Customers will respond positively and you may be surprised at the wide ranging and practical ideas you receive for becoming a leading *customer-oriented* business.

A service revolution is fast approaching. Customers are becoming tired of the poor, inattentive, uncaring, slow service provided by so many companies. Lower price travel in particular, has allowed customers to experience far higher levels of service in other countries. In California for instance, **amazing service** is the norm, not the exception.

The bottom line? Customers will desert you if you make their buying experience unpleasant; they will flock to you if you make their buying experience exceptional.

CHAPTER 23

Rapid Business Multiplier #6: Access *Other Company's Customers* To Double Your Sales, or More

There is a way to sell your product or service to customers who've never heard of you before, yet who respond in volume *as if they were your customers.*

When you employ this powerful, yet little used strategy, you gain five 'instant' advantages. You:

1. Quickly generate high-profit new sales —
    even on a tiny budget.

2. Multiply your profits without increasing
    your marketing expenditure.

3. Engineer *hundreds of percent* more sales
    from the same marketing pounds.

4. Gain powerful competitive advantage.

5. Increase your database of buying customers
    up to ten times faster.

I call this strategy **Host/Recipient** marketing. Here's how it works.

The Power of Host/Recipient Marketing

Once any business wins a new customer they have helped him or her bridge the gap between doubt, distrust, and uncertainty, to belief, trust and confidence in the product or service being offered, and themselves, the sellers.

That is why — as you have seen in earlier chapters — you will always receive a substantially higher response when you market to customers who have already bought from you, than from prospects who either have never heard of you, or have only *inquired* about what you sell.

The difference in response, as you've seen in earlier chapters, is immense — ten, or twenty+ times more sales for the same marketing cost.

But it is not only *your* customers that you can market to and receive the same high response.

Here's the secret.

If what you sell would appeal to *another company's* customers or clients — their demography being sufficiently similar to your own customers — and you were able to market your product directly to them *with the host company's personal endorsement and recommendation of you,* **you can garner the same high response you would receive as if you were marketing to your own customers.** (In this example, the 'host' is the company you approach, and you are the 'recipient'.)

Many businesses try this but fail to get a good response because they miss the key to its success. It is subtle but it makes a difference of ten or twenty times greater response.

Your offer has to be endorsed and recommended by someone of authority at the host company (chairman, managing director, or sales director, etc.) whose customers you are approaching, and the mailing must appear to have been sent by the host company themselves, not you.

Here's An Example

If your customers were business owners, and I mailed them, with your permission, a detailed promotional piece about my next seminar date, I would not receive any greater response than if I made the same offer to any other 'cold' list of business-owner prospects. Between 0.5 to 1 percent would respond.

But if I asked *you to write a letter to your customers* introducing me, plus the direct-response strategies I use to grow businesses exponentially, and you then recommended that they register for a seminar seat because of the specific business-building knowledge they will gain, you will have predisposed them to me.

When they read the information pack I send with your letter, they are likely to respond to *me* as if they were responding to *you*. Between 2 to 10 percent are likely to respond—a massive 400 percent to 1,000 percent increase in response.

Do you see the subtle difference? My offer isn't 'cold' any longer. It has become a product that **you** recommend to your customers, just as if you yourself were selling it.

How To Make Host/Recipient Marketing Work For You

Your host/recipient marketing piece must consist of the correct *elements* to make it work. Here's what your mailing envelope should include, in this order (so that the receiver first sees the host company's letter, then your letter, etc.).

1.   **A letter from the chairman, managing director, or sales director of the host company to his customers** introducing, endorsing, and recommending you, and your offer.

2.   **A sales letter from you addressed to the host company's customers** explaining the benefits of your product or service.

3.   **Your brochure or catalogue** if you have one.

4.   **Testimonials from your satisfied customers.**

5.   **An ordering device:** an order form, telephone ordering instructions, reply card. Include a reply-

paid envelope if you are asking people to order by mail.

Provide The Host With a Good Reason To Cooperate

The most effective and fairest way to arrange host/recipient alliances is to make it a worthwhile new source of profit beneficial to *both* parties.

By sharing the new profits you make from the host's customers, with the host, you forge a worthwhile and motivational partnership. When both parties have an interest in the arrangement working, more attention will be given to it.

What profit share is effective? I have found the more **generously** you share your profits the more the host will be motivated to cooperate. The more the host cooperates the more response you receive.

I share 25/75 of the gross profit with clients I arrange host/recipient alliances with—25 percent to the host, 75 percent to me, the recipient. You may think twenty-five percent is too generous. But think about it. Would *you* be motivated to spend time helping me arrange to mail an offer to your customers if I shared only 10 percent with you? You may *say* you would be but psychologically, 10 percent is not a lot.

25 percent on the other hand seems a generous share. And it is! It's enough to make the arrangement an exciting new profit source for the host company.

If *you* feel giving 25 percent of your profit away is too high, remember that it's profit you would never have if the host didn't allow you access to his or her customers, with endorsement. It's a profit-generating strategy made ten or twenty times more powerful only with the host company's involvement.

If you make an extra £100,000 profit through host/recipient alliances this year, it's profit you wouldn't have without the host's consent. Giving £25,000 to your hosts is a highly motivating amount. Do you think your hosts will want to continue the relationship next year by giving you access to their new customers? You bet! They'll be knocking on **your** door!

And £75,000 extra profit in your bank is nothing to grumble about. Giving generously creates a self-perpetuating profit centre.

How To Generate Large Profits Quickly

If you were an insurance broker, or an accountant, or a utilities supplier, or an electrician, etc. you could arrange a host/recipient alliance with your *business* clients (the hosts), to offer your services to *their* customers or clients.

Here's the scenario. Let's say you run an accountancy practise with two hundred business clients that are happy with the tax savings you have engineered for them. Each of your clients has in turn seventy customers, which gives you a 'universe' of 14,000 prospects.

Your average profit per client is £350 a year.

If you were to approach these prospects *cold*, without the host/recipient arrangement, you wouldn't want to bet on receiving more than a 0.5 percent response – 70 new clients at an average profit of £350 = £24,500 new profit.

But with a host/recipient arrangement the results are very different *for the same marketing cost.*

Now, because your offer is received with the host's endorsement and recommendation, you are likely to receive between 2 to 10 percent response. In case you accuse me of overzealous persuasion, let's say only 2 percent of the host's customers respond. Almost overnight, you have added £98,000 to your profits and gained 280 new clients (14,000 prospects x 2% = 280 x £350 = £98,000 profit.)

That's **400 percent more profit** made possible by using a host/recipient arrangement. Do you see the tremendous leverage you have with host/recipient marketing?

What would happen to your profits if you receive a larger response? Often when I arrange host/recipient marketing for my clients we receive a 5 percent, or 7 percent response, or higher. Let's look what happens if you received 5 percent.

14,000 x 5% = 700 x £350 = **£245,000 new profit.**

Suffice it to say, host/recipient marketing gives you more profit-generating leverage than any other strategy I know. You can grow your business from scratch or from an established base, faster, more profitably, at lower cost.

Do you need to gain competitive advantage? One powerful way is to use host/recipient marketing. 95 percent of your competitors do not understand the principles and philosophies I'm sharing with you. They won't be able to keep up with your growth once you apply strategies that they cannot see.

Small Business Booms With Host/Recipient Strategy

I introduced the owner of the hairdressing business I mentioned earlier to host/recipient marketing, and arranged with six companies to make an offer from her available to their customers and staff.

Within nine weeks she had received a 22 percent response, had taken bookings for the next three months, and boosted her business to a completely new level of successful trading.

The whole strategy took three hours to arrange, and I spent 45-minutes writing the letters. You can do the same. *Growing your business is straight forward if you use strategies that make your success* **predictable.**

Two Host Letters That Respond Well

Letter #1:

Here's a letter format your hosts can use to introduce you to their customers or clients (page 212). It works for any *service* business. I have written it for an accountant, but it works equally well for insurance brokers, computer consultants, electricians, painter and decorators, and so on.

Simply take the idea and rewrite it for *your* business, using the same principle appeals.

Letter #2:

This host letter is effective for selling *products* (page 213). Again, rewrite it to suit your product, using the same principal appeals.

continued on page 214...

THE HOST'S COMPANY LETTERHEAD

Dear John,

I would not usually write to you about something like this but as a good customer of mine, I want to share some information that I think could save you a substantial amount of money. So far I have saved £2,135 this year.

The person who has helped me make these savings is my accountant. His name is Robert Jones. He achieved it by recognising and reorganising areas of my profit that were not taking advantage of lower-tax opportunities the Inland Revenue itself endorses. The trouble is most companies - and unfortunately, accountants - don't have the specialised tax expertise to identify these savings possibilities. Robert is a UK tax specialist, so he knows every tax-saving opportunity.

He told me this afternoon that he is expanding his practise and has room to take on some new clients. Before he accepts clients from advertising, he asked whether any of *my* customers may like to take advantage of his service. That's why I am writing to you.

Robert has offered to give you a 40-minute initial tax-saving consultation free of charge, and without obligation. During it you'll discover if he can save you as much as he is saving his other clients, including me. If you like what he suggests, and you think he can help you more than your existing accountant, he'll give you first option on becoming a client. What's best, most of his fees are results-oriented, paid as a percentage of the extra tax savings he finds for you.

If you are not impressed with what Robert can do for you, at worst, you have lost 40-minutes of your time and discovered you are already saving maximum tax.

I highly recommend Robert as an accountant. If you would like to take his offer up phone him direct on 0123 111222 and tell him you are my customer. Let me know how it goes.

Sincerely,

Michael Newnham

Letter #1: A good 'host' letter. Wouldn't you respond to a message like this?

THE HOST'S COMPANY LETTERHEAD

Dear John,

Occasionally a product comes along that so impresses you that you want to tell as many people as possible about it!

<u>Please take 2-minutes to read this letter because I think you may be interested in what I have discovered.</u>

I buy my suits from Frasier Brothers in town, and have always been more than pleased with the fit and quality they provide at a competitive price. But last week Trevor Frasier, the owner, offered me an Italian-made, pure wool, three-piece, double-breasted suit, the quality and cut of which belongs to a £3,000 suit, but at a fraction of the price.

I normally don't think it is worth spending more than around £400 on a suit. I have found the difference in quality between a £400, and say, a £900 suit is not great enough to warrant the additional cost.

But as soon as I tried this Italian suit on, I bought it. In fact I bought *three* in case I can't get them in future!

It is lucky I got there when I did. Trevor told me he managed to buy one container of these suits from an Italian designer who had over-estimated an order for a famous London store. He was able to buy them at a considerably lower price because of this. When they are sold, he knows he won't be able to buy them again at the same price.

Because I was so impressed with them, I asked if he could wait a few days before advertising, so I could let all my customers know about them. That's why I am writing to you. If you want the chance to buy a £3,000 suit for £550, as I did, phone Trevor at Frasier Brothers right away. He's holding his advertising until Tuesday to give you first option on one or more suits.

The only thing he asked me to stipulate, which I am sure you will understand, is that he cannot give a further discount if you wanted more than one, because of the low price he has already agreed to sell them for.

Trevor's number is 0123 111 222. By the way, there is of course no obligation. If you try the suit on and don't agree it is worth the much reduced price of £550, then I apologise for getting your hopes up. But I think you'll love the quality as much as I do!

Let me know how you get on.

Sincerely,

Gary Marchant

Letter #2: Wouldn't you be tempted if you received this letter from one of your suppliers? Enough people are to make it very profitable for both host and recipient companies

How To Make Big Extra Profits From Other Companies Desperate To Sell To <u>Your</u> Customers

You can reverse the host/recipient strategy so that you become a host, and other companies become the recipient of *your* customer's business.

You gain five advantages when you become a host. You can:

1. Create a new profit-centre within your business.

2. Receive high additional profits without handling any products or providing any service.

3. Create high-profit streams of income without investing any money.

4. Provide your customers with worthwhile additional buying opportunities.

5. Work less hours for more profit.

It is simple to arrange. Contact all your customers or clients and explain the host/recipient idea to them. Tell them that for a 75/25 percent profit share in their favour, they can access **your** customers with a letter from you endorsing them and their product. You will probably need to explain the significantly larger response they can expect when marketing in this depth, because 'tradition' has taught them that making bigger, faster profits is not possible, or not ethical. Of course, the reverse is true.

So be patient, explain the process thoroughly, and help the recipient companies put a good offer together if you need to. You can then arrange an ever increasing number of high-profit host/recipient deals, year-after-year.

How To Protect Your Customer Database

What is stopping a shallow-thinking or dishonest recipient company from abusing your trust and marketing to your customers without your permission or profit share?

If you want to protect your customer database for security, or simply because you are not comfortable making your hard-earned list freely available, you can arrange for the recipient company to give you their literature, and send it directly from *your* office.

The recipient company usually pays all the costs — printing of letters, envelopes, postage. They should also pre-pack the envelopes, with your host letter included, ready for you to simply address and mail.

When customers respond, they should do so straight to the *recipient* company. In most cases this is best. Your customer then becomes the recipient's customer too, and can be marketed to freely by the recipient company in future.

Being Flexible Brings Greater Success

The point is: *be flexible.* What suits one host/recipient arrangement will not necessarily suit another. Take each one individually and make an arrangement that suits both parties well. Then you'll succeed.

Here are some alternatives you can use as a host company:

- Give your customer list straight to the recipient company to mail to directly, with the agreement that they will not use it again without your permission.

- Arrange that the recipient company provides pre-packed and stamped envelopes containing the offer they are making to your customers, *for you to address and mail.* This way you keep your database private.

- Arrange a straight 25/75 profit share in the recipient company's favour, on all the immediate orders it receives from your customers.
- Allow the customers of yours that order the

recipient company's product or service to then become that company's customer too, who they can market freely to in future.

- Arrange that all new customers the recipient company acquires through you become part of an ongoing profit-sharing asset to you both. The recipient company will give you 25 percent of all the profits it makes from your customer for life, or for a predetermined length of time.

- Protect your customer list totally by fulfilling orders yourself and ensuring you receive accurate profit share. Have the recipient's product shipped to you for fulfilment, and record the value of each order to audit the profit sharing.

Do you see the possibilities? Also, just reverse these options when you are the recipient company, rather than the host.

With flexibility and imagination, you can organise any number of high-response host/recipient alliances, and multiply your profits exponentially.

CHAPTER 24

Rapid Business Multiplier #7: Recognise The *Lifetime Value* of a Customer, And Market Accordingly

The most profitable thing you'll ever do for your business is recognise, understand, and ethically capitalize on the **lifetime value** of a customer.

What Is The Lifetime Value Of a Customer?

Most businesses look at their customers **sale by sale.** They think it's good business to try to make a profit from **every** sale. So they inject a large amount of effort and expend large amounts of cash trying to win new customers at a profit, point blank.

But there is a way you can grow your business more profitably *ten times faster.*

Realise this. Once you win a new customer and they buy from you for the first time, and then you nurture your relationship with that person by regularly communicating and offering additional buying opportunities in an ethical, respectful, interesting, and educational manner, that customer becomes a member of your extended business 'family'.

Winning new customers — as you've seen in earlier chapters — is the most expensive thing a business ever does. But once you *have* won a new customer, that person will, and **wants to,** buy from you and recommend others to you **repeatedly** in the weeks, months, and years ahead.

The lifetime value of a customer is the total profit worth of that customers purchasing over the 'lifetime' of your relationship.

How To Recognise The Lifetime Value of Your Customers

Let's say you own a business selling men's suits and accessories. Your average sale, which consists of one suit plus two residual items — a tie and a shirt, or cuff links and a belt — is £250 from which you make £125 gross profit.

On average, each customer returns two times a year so your gross profit per customer is £250 a year.

Each customer remains a patron of your business for an average five years.

It costs you £20 to acquire every new customer (you run an advert costing £500 and you get 25 sales = £20 per customer.)

So the lifetime value of your customer is **1,230** (£250 gross profit per year x 5 years, minus £20 acquisition cost = £1,230).

Every Time You Invest £20 You Make £1,230

In other words, every time you invest £20 in advertising you get a profit return of £1,230. Knowing this, you would want to keep investing as many £20's as you can! Each time you do, you earn another £1,230.

Why Setting a Fixed Marketing Budget Will Stunt Your Profits

To grow your business faster you have to recognise the lifetime value of your customer. Then you will want to invest as many £20's in advertising as you can **now,** realising that on average, every new customer will earn you £1,230.

The biggest marketing mistake you can make is to set a fixed marketing budget. If you do you will seriously stunt your profits.

Here's why.

If you view your advertising as bringing in **'only 25 new sales'** at £105 net profit each (£125 minus £20 customer acquisition cost), and you advertise twice a month, so you make £5,250 gross profit a month (two ads produce 50 new customers at £105 net profit = £5,250), it appears—after deducting overheads and peripheral costs—**that you only have a limited amount of funds left to advertise and market your business with;** say, 20 percent of your £5,250 monthly gross profit = £1050.

Your ads cost £500 each. So you think you are limited to two adverts a month. Every accountant and every bank manager I've ever met instructs businesses to calculate their marketing budgets this way. But it's a mirage—and a costly mistake.

Pay For SALES, Not Advertising

If you set an advertising budget, you are paying for a fixed limited number of advertisements from which you hope to produce profitable sales.

But you should never pay for advertising. You should only pay for **sales.**

When you recognise that each £20 you spend on advertising is 'buying' you the most valuable asset you will ever have— a customer, and the lifetime value of that customer, in this case £1,230—you will never again be content just paying for advertising (fixing an advertising budget).

Pay for sales! If a customer is worth £1,230 over his or her lifetime patronage of your business, and costs you £20 to acquire, you would be foolish not to increase your advertising budget to produce as many £20 customers as you can.

Do you see the **monumental growth opportunity** the lifetime value of a customer provides you with?

But this is just the beginning. Let's look at some greater possibilities.

How To Gain 'Instant' Competitive Advantage And Scoop 100's - 1,000's of New Customers

Almost every business I see tries to make a profit on **every** sale.

219

Businesses energetically vie with their competitors to win custom-ers money. From this bombardment of sales messages customers have to weigh one sales offer against other often very similar of-fers and choose the one they think will most benefit them.

But there is an easier — and markedly more effective — method of attracting customers, and simultaneously gaining powerful com-petitive advantage.

It's revealed when you look at the lifetime-value philoso-phy a little deeper.

If, on average, each customer's lifetime value is £1,230 then in theory you could spend £1,229 acquiring him or her, and still be £1 in profit! Of course you want to make substantially more than £1 per customer but do you see the opportunity you have?

At present you are spending £20 to acquire a £1,230-profit customer. But dozens of other companies are spending a similar amount vying for the same customer's money.

Now, because you recognise the lifetime value each cus-tomer is worth to you, your marketing possibilities open right up. It now makes sense to spend £100, £200, £500 or more, ac-quiring **multitudes more customers**, and still make a profit of £1,130, £1,030, or £700 respectively.

You Can Create 10-Times More Marketing Leverage

If overnight you have 10-times the marketing power at your dis-posal by increasing your budget from £20 per customer to £200, you have 10-times the might to win more new customers. You have created **massive marketing leverage** that will bring a fast influx of profit-generating sales.

Make Your Offer *Irresistible* To Capture Masses Of New Customers

With ten times or more marketing pounds in your kitty you can create an offer that has such high perceived value that custom-ers cannot resist responding — in their masses.

Here are just some ways you can invest your increased mar-keting budget and attract an influx of new customers:

- Increase the size and effectiveness of your advertising.
- Offer a two-for-one introductory purchase.
- Offer a three-for-one introductory purchase.
- Offer to 'buy' £100 worth of additional products or service for your customer for every £50 he spends.
- Offer a £100 gift voucher, good for the next 12-months, with every £50 purchase.
- Offer a £200 gift voucher for every £50 purchase.
- Offer a 50% introductory discount.
- Offer an 80% or 90% introductory discount.
- Offer a 'ridiculous' introductory price on any product or service:

   - a £300 suit for £20
   - a £20 haircut for £2
   - a £40-a-head meal for £2.50
   - a £2,000 computer for £500
   - 30-days free calls for switching telephone providers.

and so on, ad infinitum. You see the possibilities.

If you owned a tailoring shop, and you ran a quarter-page or half-page advert, and you announced that you had received a shipment of beautifully cut, £500 Italian suits that you were selling for £50 to the first one hundred customers who came in, and you gave a believable reason-why you were selling them at that low price, and you provided a strong risk-reversal guarantee to eliminate any doubt customers may have over the authenticity of your offer, do you think you would pull customers away from your competitors? You can believe it!

Let's say the cost price of each £500 suit is £250. You're selling for £50 so your net cost is £200, plus the £20 cost-per-customer for the ad (assuming the ad is the same size) = £220 total cost. £1,250 lifetime value of each customer, minus £220 cost is £1,030. In one marketing move you have attracted one hundred new customers worth a total lifetime value of £103,000 profit (100 x £1,030.)

In other words, by placing just ten adverts you could generate well over £1,000,000 worth of profit (£1,030,000) while your competitors are left wondering how on earth you can afford to sell £500 suits for £50.

NOTE: If you advertised an offer like the above, some or many of your *existing* customers would see it and want the same deal. What do you do? One of two things.

First, if you do advertise your offer give your existing customers the same deal! Not all of them will want to take it up because no matter how 'good' the offer, it won't suit them. But the customers who do take it up are simply **adding** to their lifetime value, not reducing it. Why? Because the more you offer your existing customers extraordinary buying opportunities **the more they will patronize you.** Don't think of the lifetime value of a customer as being set in stone. You can **increase** the lifetime value of customers the more you communicate favourable service (see Chapter 19).

Write to your existing customers *before* your special-offer appears, telling them what you will be advertising, and offering them first choice to buy.

Second, you can make your offer 'invisible' to your existing customers by making it available to targeted prospects on a host/recipient basis instead of by advertising.

If you owned a restaurant, and you knew that on average couples order a meal worth £60, from which you make £40 gross profit, and they return every six weeks, and their patronage of your restaurant lasts two years, the lifetime value of your customer is **£680 gross profit** (£40 x 17 meals over two years = £680.)

Rather than attracting new customers incrementally by marketing your restaurant like every other restaurant does, you could 'gift' dinners to attract **masses of customers** in no time.

How? You could make available 100 £60 dinners for £2.50 per head to targeted prospective long-term customers. As long as they are cutout demographically for becoming a lifetime customer, you could send a targeted mailing, or organise a host/recipient alliance with appropriate companies, with a valuable-looking invitation for a £2.50 or complimentary evening meal for two. If you had the cash to fund the initial cost, you could provide 1,000 to 2,000 complimentary meals to targeted customers over a one month period. You'd instantly write up £680,000 to £1,360,000 worth of profit from one month's marketing because each couple's lifetime value is £680.

Do you see the vast possibilities you have? Do you understand the potential your business has when you recognise the lifetime value of your customer?

Almost any business can skyrocket their profits and gain almost *unfair* competitive advantage from this philosophy. If it is not immediately obvious how you can apply it to your business, think again.

If, for instance, you sell a one-shot product such as double glazing, you can organise high-profit host/recipient, recipient/host alliances with other companies.

In this case the lifetime value calculation is based on the profits you gain by selling to *other companies customers*, or the 25% profit share you gain by allowing other companies to sell to *your customers.* Remember what I said in Chapter One—**you** make the rules. **You** can influence every sales process, marketing strategy, promotional event, advertising campaign in **your favour.** As long as what you do is legal and ethical, you can do whatever you like to lure, endear, and compel customers or clients to *your* business or practice, in favour of your competitors'.

One of the greatest rapid business-multiplying strategies you can adopt is the lifetime value principal. Calculate, understand, and apply lifetime value marketing to every customer or client acquisition move you now make. By doing so, you release the full, geometric growth and wealth-generating capability of your business, which—*without* lifetime value marketing—is impossible to tap.

Apply Lifetime Value marketing to your business **today!**

PART 5

3 Bonus Chapters

BONUS CHAPTER 1

How To Put Your Business On A New Course Of Success In 30 Days Or Less

What can you do if your business or practice is slow? If it isn't generating the volume of sales you want—and need—to grow, prosper, and become competitively formidable?

First, know that you *can* turn your business around rapidly—within a matter of weeks.

Second, analyse how you are currently approaching your market:

- What are you doing to **seduce** your customers or clients to buy?
- How **pro-active** are you in attracting new customers?
- How **innovative** are your sales offers?
- How **customer-oriented** is your marketing approach?
- Are you applying **direct-response** strategies to every approach you make? Or are you frittering cash resources on ineffectual institutional marketing?

Compel Customers To Buy From You Now!

The secret of attracting virtually as many customers or clients as you can handle is to **develop** *relationships* **with them.**

Does that ring a bell? It should by now!

Developing relationships with your customers or clients means **communicating** compellingly and regularly with them, making every transaction an **enjoyable and memorable** experience, offering interesting, beneficial, and preferential **buying opportunities,** offering informative and innovative **choices** to help people make wise buying decisions, **thanking** customers for their purchase.

Look at how most businesses *you* buy from treat customers. You can relatively easily surpass their service, can't you? When you do, you become a champion in the eyes of your customers.

As soon as you develop consistent, meaningful, **value-based** buyer-seller relationships with people your business will change forever — and success will follow.

Think about most businesses *lack* of relationship building. When was the last time you received a personalised letter from your local clothes shop telling you about the new range of casual suits they've just taken delivery of and how much they would like you to come along in the next 14 days for a private fitting?

When did you last receive a personal invitation to spend a romantic weekend at the elegant hotel you and your partner stayed at a few months ago?

Or an invitation to celebrate your wedding anniversary at your favourite Italian restaurant?

When have you walked out of a shop, or car dealership, or restaurant, or supermarket, or bank and thought, "That was an enjoyable and memorable experience?"

How often have you received a letter or card in the post thanking you for your purchase from a store, hairdresser, solicitor, accountant, bank, dentist? In fact, have you *ever* received a "thank you" note from *any* company or practice you bought from — even those you spent many thousands of pounds with, like estate agents, car dealers, travel agents, building firms, computer dealers?

If you have, you're lucky. Not one in twenty businesses realise the rapid-growth significance of these simple **but powerful** relationship-building methods.

Communicate Regularly By Mail And Make A Fortune

The most sales-effective method of consistently communicating with your customers is to do so by **mail.**

As you systematically attract and acquire new customers and regularly mail new, interesting, beneficial buying opportunities to them, your sales — and profits — will increase rapidly.

Some business owners say to me "It is not worth making the

effort to mail regular offers because only 3, or 5, or 10 percent of customers respond."

Realise that "only" 3, 5, or 10 percent response is *where your fortune lies.*

That 'small' percentage response is worth thousands, tens of thousands, or hundreds of thousands in additional profits to you as you keep mailing new buying opportunities.

My publisher, Big Sur, recently mailed a subscription offer to my monthly newsletter — *Business Success Newsletter* — to their customer list. The mailing resulted in a 15.9 percent response and generated a large income within days of the letter being posted.

You can create similar results in your business!

But that's just the start. Let's look deeper.

A Simple Marketing Lesson That Can Make You Rich

Because a customer doesn't respond to one offer you make available doesn't mean he or she will not respond to *another.*

Non-responders simply present a new selling opportunity.

By **not** responding, your customer is simply saying, "This *particular* offer doesn't fit my current needs or desires," or "I am not able to take advantage of it *this time,*" or "I can't *afford* it at the moment."

Very rarely does a customer think, "Oh no, not another darn mailing from ABC company!"

As long as you communicate with a sincere, interesting, benefit-oriented, non-pushy approach, your customers or clients **enjoy** receiving buying opportunities from you.

Have you ever bought a book or CD from a mail order club? Do you look forward to receiving the monthly selection? Of course! Because you *enjoy* reading and listening to music. As long as the club sends intelligent offers based on your buying history you will count the days until their next selection arrives.

Will you buy every time? Probably not. But that doesn't mean you want the club to stop sending offers. You will buy **periodically** — and keep adding to the club's profits.

Have a look at Amazon (www.amazon.co.uk). Get on-line and buy a book or CD from Amazon and see how smart they are. Their site demonstrates a marketing lesson that will make you rich when you apply it to your business.

When you make a book or CD selection from Amazon three or four or five *other* books or CD's in **your category of interest** are automatically listed.

I recently bought *The Mirror Makers* by Stephen Fox (the best history of advertising and its creators I've read). As soon as I selected the title a headline appeared on screen announcing — "Customers who bought this book also bought:" Four **related** titles were listed, plus a 'link' to even more suggestions if I wanted to view them.

Are these suggestions helpful? Certainly. Most customers find them interesting *because they are targeted to their category of interest.*

Are they profitable for Amazon? You bet! On average, up to 30 percent of customers decide to buy a second or third title simply because targeted suggestions were made. (I bought a second title I never would have if it hadn't been suggested.)

Keep in mind, if a customer does not buy it is usually for one of only four reasons:

1. They don't **want** or have **no need** for that particular offer.
2. It is not a suitable **time** for them to respond — for any personal, family, or business reason.
3. They feel your offer will not sufficiently solve their **problem** or provide the promised **result**.
4. They cannot **afford** the price.

Almost every customer you acquire **wants** to buy from you again — and repeatedly — when what you offer meets with their current desires or needs. Different offers suit different people at different times. When you understand that you *keep communicating* different and targeted buying opportunities to all your customers all the time to provide each person with the widest and wisest buying opportunities.

When 3-15 percent of your customers respond to a particular offer — and 85-97 percent don't — that's great! You make money on the 3-15 percent — often a large amount of money.

The remaining eighty-five to ninety-seven percent are saying, figuratively, "Not this time, thank you, but please continue informing me of new, interesting buying opportunities!"

When you then develop, improve, modify, expand, add-onto,

or package your products or services and continually introduce them to your customers, your sales and profits will skyrocket.

Aim To Repeatedly Sell To 100% Of Your Customers!

My customer philosophy is different from most. I take the attitude that my client never wants me to stop sending opportunities to improve their results or fill their desires or needs with products or services I provide — unless they *ask* me to stop.

Your customers haven't inquired or bought from you without reason. People respond to an offer *because they appreciate the particular benefit or value you provide*.

In other words, they are **highly receptive** to the type of product, service, or treatment you sell or administer.

If a customer does not respond to a particular offer you extend it does **not** mean their interest has lapsed. It simply means that that particular offer isn't suitable for them — for one of the four reasons I explained. But a *different* offer could be.

So by continually making new, different, thoughtful, **targeted** offers to your list, you gradually sell more and more to more and more customers. Or gradually convert more and more inquirers to buyers.

Another point: **You** — or **I** — cannot predetermine what will most benefit your customers. You must *ask them*. How do you ask? You extend a targeted buying opportunity. You then track and analyse the response.

If response is "high" your customers are telling you, "This offer is valuable to me, it is a suitable time for me, and the price is right for me. Thank you — I'll buy!"

If response is "low" your customers are telling you, "This offer is not right for me, or it's not a suitable time, or the price is out of reach. But please continue informing me of other offers."

11 Ways To Rapidly Boost Sales

Here are 11 strategies that will boost your sales and generate rapid new profits.

1. Communicate regularly with your existing customers.

Developing a successful business is no different from developing a successful romantic relationship, or close family, or intimate circle of friends. It relies on *regular, quality communication.*

You would not expect to develop a close family relationship if you hardly spoke to one another.

You wouldn't expect a personal relationship to be more than a fleeting association without regular, interest*ing* and interest*ed* communication.

Your closest friends are the friends you talk to most *often* and with most meaning.

Regular, quality communication builds meaningful and lasting relationships — no matter in what arena.

Customers or clients are *people!* Develop quality buyer/seller relationships with those people. Communicate often. Recognise customers' special occasions and other important dates. Make them feel special. Let them know they are a member of your extended business family. Look after them. Address their wants and needs.

When you do, they will respond by buying more of whatever it is you sell. And they will enthusiastically recommend you to their family, friends and colleagues.

2. Target your sales message.

Every customer or client has personal preferences when they buy any product or service.

Tom next door might only buy low-cost shoes. You only buy the finest Italian soft leather shoes. That's *your personal preference.* And has nothing to do with what Tom buys.

If you come into my shoe store and buy a pair of the finest Italian loafers I have available, and I then mail you details about my latest, lowest-cost range, I'm wasting your time — and mine. Tom will be interested in my mailing and may well buy some shoes from me. But you won't.

Whatever it is you sell, record what your customers or clients buy and then tailor your communication to *their* individual interests and desires.

A good database programme makes an easy job of capturing your customer's buying histories and mail merging personalised buying opportunities. No business should operate without a computerized database these days. A database is the keystone of your business success because it makes **relationship marketing** a reality — for even the tiniest business.

Regularly target your customers or clients with new offers and opportunities and you will rapidly optimize your sales revenue and bottom line profits.

3. Attract new customers or clients by increasing your marketing POWER.

Are there additional ways you can reach target prospective customers? There probably are. Finding them will instantly *increase your marketing power.*

A client asked me how to increase sales without increasing his financial risk. He did not — rightly — want to splash out on larger advertising, a larger brochure, or a telesales operation. At least, not until he had tested each approach. But testing takes time and he wanted to increase his customer acquisition programme now.

He was running small ads in two newspapers and receiving a reasonably profitable stream of new customers each week. His ads were making money! So I advised him to simply do **more** of what he was doing already — place **more** small ads in **more** publications. It sounds simple. *But he wasn't doing it.*

He assumed that because other publications didn't have as high a circulation they wouldn't be worth advertising in. But circulation alone doesn't matter. The *only* two things that matter — in this case — are: One, does your advertising reach your targeted audience? Two, does it make money?

If a targeted ad which costs £1,000, and brings in £3,000 profit, is run in a smaller circulation paper, costs £500, and makes only £1,500 in new profits instead of £3,000, is it worth running?

Of course! It generates a 200% growth on your investment! (£1,500 gross profit, minus £500 ad cost = £1,000 = 200% growth on your £500 investment).

It doesn't matter that you normally make £2,000 profit on

231

the same ad in a larger circulation paper. One thousand pounds profit from a different paper is **additional profit** and **additional new customers gained.**

My client followed this advice, repeated his tested ads in seven additional papers and magazines, and has now more than *doubled* his sales within just a few weeks.

How can **you** increase your marketing power without increasing your risk? Here are five suggestions:

- Advertise in more papers that reach your target prospective customers — *with tested ads.*
- Advertise in more magazines that reach your target prospective customers — *with tested ads.*
- Increase your cold mailings — *with tested mailers.*
- Increase your field sales calls — *with tested approaches.*
- Increase your telemarketing calls — *with tested scripts.*

4. Apply lifetime value marketing.

Read, reread, and read again — and then *immediately apply* — my advice on Lifetime Value marketing — Chapter 24, page 217. It is the secret of creating unbounded success and riches in virtually any business or professional practice you can name.

5. Arrange high-profit host/recipient alliances with non-competing businesses.

Host/recipient marketing provides you with massive growth leverage. How? It gives you access to other company's customers or clients *as if they were your own.*

I have written about how to generate large new profits through host/recipient marketing earlier in the book.

But I've discovered an interesting challenge. Many business owners who consult with me after reading the book have never tried to arrange host/recipient alliances. This is strange because I explain it is one of the most powerful marketing strategies you can use in business. Imagine! You are able to accelerate sales by up to tenfold or more for a **fraction** of the cost you'd normally have to outlay to acquire the same increase in revenue.

Why don't more business owners pursue this strategy?

The answer is that host/recipient alliances take a little effort to arrange. But that effort pays BIG dividends!

Develop the millionaire mind-set of constantly identifying and marketing to **the most probable area of highest response.** If one strategy provides you with considerably *greater response* for the same or less effort, time and cost, pursue it like a bloodhound.

I have made more money — more rapidly — through arranging host/recipient alliances than through any other strategy. I urge you to do the same! — see page 206.

6. Ask for referrals.

Referrals generate easy sales! Write to all your existing customers or clients and offer a worthwhile discount, gift or reward when they introduce a friend, associate or peer.

Offer the referred person an **irresistible** first time buying or take-up opportunity to maximise response.

If you are a professional and you feel giving a direct reward or gift is professionally sensitive or unethical, just *ask* for referrals. As long as your clients or patients receive tangible benefit from the service or treatment you provide, they will usually be more than happy to refer people. But you have to *ask.*

How do you ask? Simply write a personal letter explaining that you are expanding your practice and have room to take on (x-number) of new clients. Before you approach the outside market you thought it would be a nice gesture to first offer your best clients the opportunity of introducing people they know to the same level of service and results they are receiving from your practice. If they know of a friend, associate or peer who might like to benefit, you will be pleased to provide an introductory, no-obligation initial consultation or review to discover if you can help. "Please ask the person you refer to call (telephone number) by (date)."

This approach works effectively to bring you a constant stream of targeted new customers or clients.

Another approach is to ask for referrals on the back of business reply envelopes (BRE's). I suggested my publisher try this with BRE's included with the sales letter for my book. They produce a steady five percent response — 5 percent referrals we would never have if we didn't ask, and which cost us nothing to generate!

7. Arrange a special event.

You have almost limitless opportunities to draw new customers or clients with special events. What works? Almost anything out of the ordinary — with one proviso: it must be fun and interesting, or it must have value.

Here are 11 special events clients have used with great success:

- Open evenings to preview new stock or a new service.
- Preferential invitations to privately view a new range or opportunity.
- Test drives or other "live" test or trial experiences.
- A live in-store or in-factory demonstration.
- Personal appearances by designers, supplier chairmen or managing directors.
- Celebrity launches.
- Celebration buffets.
- Games of chance.
- Skills contests.
- Special occasion promotions.
- Visits to manufacturers.

You can use virtually *any* reason to stage an event. Put a pen to paper and let ideas flow. The more events you hold — and the more informative, inventive, fun or valuable they are — the more customers or clients you'll draw.

8. Acquire mailing lists of qualified prospects.

Buying mailing lists of targeted prospective buyers is a powerful customer acquisition and sales-growth device. You can pinpoint with laser accuracy those customers or clients who actively buy your category of product or service — and present your most persuasive sales proposition to them via direct mail.

The key to mailing list success is to spend the time targeting accurately, test systematically, then roll-out your marketing on the results of your most responsive test.

If you sold investment opportunities, for instance, you would obtain lists of people who **have already** invested, have done so **recently** — during the last six to twelve months ideally — have done so **frequently,** and have invested **most money.** These people are active investors and are the most likely to be interested in more investment opportunities.

This time-honoured **recency/frequency/monetary** formula is the best model to follow. (It says that the category of product or service people *have* recently bought, they will likely buy *more of quite quickly.* It is a reliable protocol.)

People you would avoid are those who have only shown *interest* in investing but have not *actually* invested. These people are a far more difficult sell.

I would explore and adopt a vigorous direct mailing strategy for your business right away.

9. Give payment options.

You will increase your sales by up to 30 percent or more by accepting credit card payments.

You will increase your sales by 90 percent or more by offering payments by instalment — spread over a number of weeks or months. The higher the ticket price the more sales increase with instalment options.

10. Offer a "buy-back" guarantee on high ticket products.

Business owners often ask me what they can do to maintain sales during a recession. One powerful strategy I advise them to adopt is a **buy-back guarantee.**

People worry about being short of money — or losing their jobs — during a recession. So they cut back their buying. A buy-back guarantee helps alleviate their fear.

How does it work? You guarantee to buy-back the product within one, two or three years at an attractive market price.

Will you lose out? Or worse, put *yourself* at risk?

Let's see. Let's say you are a car dealer. You find many prospective car buyers are delaying purchasing because they are worried about their future finances. So you guarantee to buy-back their car within one to three years at a good price.

Let's say your average car sale is £12,000 and your gross margin 17 percent—£2,040.

Let's also say that, conservatively, your sales increase by 30 percent on the strength of your guarantee, the media coverage it attracts, and the competitive advantage you gain. (Your sales could increase substantially more then 30 percent with a buy-back guarantee.)

Your dealership used to sell 50 cars a month, so now you sell 65 (30% increase). The additional 15 car sales make you an extra £30,600 profit a month—£367,200 a year. Not bad.

But then, as recession hits harder, 20 percent of customers decide to take up your buy-back guarantee. Every month 13 cars are returned (65 cars sold x 20% = 13). Let's say, on average, a generous market value for the returned cars is 70% of the original purchase price. That is £8,400 (£12,000 x 70% = £8,400).

So you buy back 13 cars each month at a cost of £109,200 (13 x £8,400 = £109,200). What do you do with them?

You resell them on the used market—at a price more people feel comfortable risking. You settle for making 5 - 10 percent margin to move the cars quickly. With a good, direct-response marketing campaign you should find buyers rapidly.

Let's say you add 5 percent. On an average £8,400 buy-back cost, that's £420 profit on a sale price of £8,820 (£8,400 + 5% = £8,820). 13 cars x 12 months x £420 profit is £65,520 additional profit per year.

Adding it all up. Your sales increased by 30% when you offered the buy-back guarantee, making you an extra £367,200 profit a year. You resell the 13 returned cars every month for an additional £65,520 profit a year.

A total extra profit per year of £432,720.

That's good. But what happens if you can't make a margin on the resold cars? Will you lose out? No—you just won't make as *much* total extra profit. Does it matter? You have already increased your profits by £367,200 a year. Do you care if you simply recoup the £8,400 you pay for each buy-back car? I wouldn't. The word-of-mouth advertising you'd receive would generate more profits than you would ever 'lose' because you are generous with your customers.

Do you see the possibilities? It is difficult to lose when you offer customer-friendly buying opportunities and extraordinary value.

How can you apply the buy-back strategy to your product? Get a pen and calculate a few alternatives. You'll be surprised what possibilities you discover.

One caveat: as with any marketing strategy, test and fine-tune the buy-back strategy before you launch it full swing. And, of course, to make it work you need good cash flow. Don't over-stretch your cash resources. (If you are applying the strategies in this book you will quickly be in a cash-rich position.)

11. Test, test, test!

If you ask me if any of my clients ever fail to grow their business by large degrees, the answer is **Yes!**

If you ask me if any of my clients who **consistently apply** the strategies I teach ever fail to grow by large degrees, the answer is **No!**

You can become a virtual marketing genius — achieving quantum growth, while your competitors are left looking on in awe — when you understand and apply — to everything you do — the preeminent strategy of **testing.**

Test alternative headlines, opening gambits, offers, ads, letters, guarantees, prices, payment terms, premiums, bonuses, mailing lists, telesales and field-sales approaches — one versus another. You will invariably discover that one approach or method outpulls another by margins of 50 - 1000 percent, or more. Most businesses never test. So they fail to learn which approach their market responds to most.

I showed a client how to test two different approaches on a split-run mailing (half = approach #1, half = approach #2). One produced **29 percent higher response** than the other. If he hadn't tested he would never have discovered that more effective approach. And never generated the 29 percent higher sales for no additional cost of marketing.

Always test everything you do. Then roll-out your winning approaches to grow your business rapidly.

BONUS CHAPTER 2

How To Find Up To £1,000,000 New "Cash" To Rapidly Increase Your Sales

What would you do to improve your sales if I gave you £10,000? Or *tens* of thousands? Or even a lump sum that eludes most business owners all their life: one million pounds cash?

Well, I'm going to — figuratively. The information in this chapter is as good as crisp new notes drawn from the bank.

First, let's set the scene.

Virtually every day I see business men and women — and their employees — rack their brains, exert their energy, and spend cash all with one main purpose: **to find new customers.**

Yet ninety-five percent of their efforts are largely wasted. They invest £1,000, £5,000, £10,000, £100,000 or more, but that investment is hard-pushed to make a profit.

Why? Because **where** they invest it, and **how** they employ it (the effectiveness of their strategy or the skill of their advertising copy, for instance) is not **capable** of generating an immediate and high response.

Put differently, ninety-five pounds out of every one hundred put into growing most businesses is usually unlikely to result in exciting growth. And certainly unlikely to propel the owner of that business toward success and a personal fortune.

When I visit a new client the first thing I do is look for "hidden assets" in the business.

In virtually every case, I find assets, possibilities and untapped resources the business owner hasn't recognised, which —

when leveraged — rapidly generate a cash windfall of £10,000 to £1,000,000, or more.

I would wager it is true of **your** business or practice.

Let me share one of the most frequently under-utilised assets I discover — the ability to 'buy' tens of thousands or millions of pounds worth of advertising with 'cash' most business owners never realise they have.

Of course, I'm talking about **FREE PUBLICITY!**

For a reason I don't understand, most business owners never seriously pursue publicity. Those who do, receive thousands upon thousands of pounds of advertising that brings in untold levels of new sales and profits — for free!

A client who sells solid oak furniture called me wanting to know if he could get further mileage on a strategy I introduced him to a year ago. That single strategy has already brought him *hundreds* of new customers, at a cost of just a few hundred pounds a year.

What is the strategy? I advised him to **educate** his customers — and prospective customers — on the skilled and fascinating process of oak furniture construction and craftsmanship.

Rather than simply expecting customers to walk into his store and buy an expensive piece of furniture after not much more than *looking* at it, and having to *trust* what the salesperson tells him about its quality — as virtually every furniture store expects customers to do — I advised my client to invite customers to **witness** the furniture building process by taking them to the factories which manufactured and supplied his stock.

Customers responded to these invitations by the score and appreciate the opportunity he provides. The result? He is winning *hundreds* of additional sales he couldn't attract before.

How could he get *more* leverage from this strategy? Simple. Produce a press release to attract dozens or hundreds *more* customers he is not able to reach through advertising.

It took me 20-minutes to write a 400-word press release. It took him one hour to fax it to various papers and magazines.

A few weeks later this note arrived in the post:

"Dear Paul,

Overleaf is press release result! Excellent response to this —

239

thank you! Trip itself went astonishingly well—we took 30 people—12 orders for £25,000 at a profit of £13,500. Customers paid for the costs of the trip—coach/hotel/courier/shuttle. Marketing cost: around £3,000, but this also generated **another** £30,000 worth of turnover. Marvellous! Next trip to Belgium 9/10th September. Regards, Nick."

That's the power of press releases. Nick will repeatedly win new customers as he creates new and interesting ways to sell his furniture—and produces press releases to announce them.

What would it cost Nick to "buy" the same amount of advertising space? About £3,000 a time. Would he attract the same level of response if he were to buy space and publish "adverts", rather than having an editorial written about him? Probably not. So the £3,000 cost of the space is more likely equivalent to a space three or four times the size—at a cost of maybe £6,000-£10,000—to pull the same response.

In other words, Nick receives six to ten thousand pounds worth of advertising each time a press release is published—without a penny leaving his bank account. Do you think that has a geometrically high affect on his bottom line profits? You bet!

It is simple to publicize your business, get thousands of pounds worth of free advertising every week or month, and attract a constant stream of new, buying customers.

How To Get Up To £1 Million Pounds Or More Worth Of FREE Publicity For Your Business Each Year

In order to get free publicity you must either:

1. Be newsworthy.
2. Be controversial or outrageous.
3. Have a "pet" subject.
4. Have an unusual "angle."
5. Solve a problem.
6. Be eccentric.

Here's a quick course primer on each of the six.

Be Newsworthy

Have you developed from scratch — or improved — a product or service that creates a notable advancement on anything already existing in your market?

If so, it is newsworthy!

A former soccer professional who retired early with a back injury developed an advanced bed and mattress system that helped *cure* his back after years of pain.

A kitchen company sourced and imported a range of European fitted kitchens that are better made, and provide more value pound for pound than any other kitchen you can buy in the UK.

A software company developed the most powerful and flexible accounting software you can use in business today.

A young entrepreneur launched an innovative door-to-door grocery delivery service.

Nick Smith decided to show customers the furniture building process rather than expect them to just buy on sight.

The list goes on. Can *your* product or service be included in this list? If so, you can attract free press coverage.

The point is this: None of these business owners **recognised** their product or service as being 'special' enough to attract media coverage.

If this is you — or to be more succinct — if you haven't attracted £10,000 to £1,000,000 worth of free publicity during the last twelve months, **recognise that you easily <u>can</u>.**

If you have made *any* innovation, or developed *any* new product or service that has tangible and recognizable value and benefit to customers, the likelihood is you have a **newsworthy** item. *Pursue* media coverage. *Recognise* the interest targeted readers, listeners and viewers will have in what you've developed — and therefore the eagerness of the press to publish articles about you.

Be Controversial

Remember what happened with the controversial potency pill, Viagra? Even *before* it was on the market it attracted millions of pounds worth of free publicity which created instant demand.

Remember Victor Kiam, the man who was so impressed with the razor, he bought the company?

You may not have a 'Viagra' or a 'Remington'. But if you have any type of controversial product or service, or a controversial **claim** about what you sell or do, you can attract big media coverage.

Ripe for controversy are subjects on or linked to:

- Love
- Sex
- Money
- Fear
- Gender differences
- Health/Weight
- Politics

You can make a controversial **claim** about almost any subject. One caveat: make **sure** you can back it up.

Look at this. If I sent a press release claiming:

"Expert Helps Business Owners Make Up To £10,000 - £1,000,000 In 90-Days Or Less"

...and I then explained why I am qualified to make that claim, and gave examples to back it up, do you think I'd attract attention in the business press?

If you invented a lawn mower that was 100% powered by daylight, and you faxed the press a release stating:

"New Lawn mower Powered By Daylight Only – No More Cables Or Noisy Petrol Engines"

...and you explained how your new lawn mower worked and the benefits to gardeners, do you think the media would cover your story?

The likelihood is high – because the media are continually looking for stories that will attract more readers. Controversial or outrageous claims – as long as they can be backed up – always attract high readership.

Here are more controversial and outrageous claims:

**"Expert Reveals How Anyone Can Make
16-21% Annual Return On Their Investment,
With Only Small Risk"**

**"Man Solves Car Exhaust Pollution—
New Converter Emits Fumes Cleaner Than Air"**

**"Mother Discovers How To Make Babies
Sleep Through The Night"**

**"Psychologist Discovers Secret Of Attracting
The Opposite Sex—at Will "**

**"Hypnotherapist Cures Smokers
of Lifetime Habit In 30-Minutes Or Less"**

I could give you dozens more examples. The point is, all these subjects have an element of controversy or outrageousness linked to them.

Make a "wild" claim about your particular product or service, package it in a press release, make sure you can back up your claim, and you're almost guaranteed to receive some worthwhile and profitable media coverage!

Have A "Pet" Subject

In 1977, Art L. Williams started a life insurance company. Not any life insurance company. But a company that pays out *only* on death. Unusual? Yes. He did it because "death" insurance became his "pet" subject—or "crusade" as Art calls it.

After years of paying into a life insurance policy, his mother, who was the breadwinner of the family, died at a tragically young age, leaving behind Art, his brothers and sisters, and their Dad. Mr Williams, Senior, understandably assumed the life insurance policy they had been paying into for years would provide the family with a decent lump sum on which to live.

He was mistaken. They were given, as memory serves me, a sum of only $10,000 — a meagre amount above the value of the premiums they had paid into the policy. They would have been better off investing the same money in a low-return high street savings account.

The upshot? Art and his family were not only devastated by the death of his mother but also left on the brink of poverty without her income. Art was furious that life insurance companies could get away with charging hefty premiums, yet pay out measly sums because of a tricky clause relating to the 'time' of death.

It became his crusade. In 1977 Art opened the **A.L. Williams Life Insurance Company.** His promise was that when you pay into *his* policy your family will be **guaranteed** a substantial and predetermined lump sum on your death.

He was — and is today — *passionate* about his ethical policy. It genuinely helps, supports and provides security for families at a time of grievance and need.

He relentlessly publicised his crusade. As a result, *thousands* of press articles were written about him and his new, 'death only' policy. He was invited onto *hundreds* of TV and radio shows in America. To even attempt calculating the total dollar-worth of all the free publicity he gained would be nigh impossible. It runs into the *tens of millions.*

Within 10 years of launching its new policy, A.L. Williams Life Insurance Company was not only out-selling Prudential — the biggest insurance company in the world at the time — but **several** of America's largest life insurance companies **combined.**

That's the power of having a "pet" subject.

If something *nags, irritates, annoys* or *angers* you enough, you can bet **other** people feel the same way. Make it your pet subject. **Determine** to improve the product or service — and make people's lives easier or help them attain superior value.

The opposite is just as appealing — if you are passionate about a 'positive' subject, make it your pet subject. Then enthusiastically tell the world! The media will usually be interested.

Have An Unusual 'Angle'

Almost any product or service can have an unusual 'angle' tagged to it. It just takes a little imagination and brainstorming.

What if you owned a deep-muscle massage clinic – how could you create an unusual angle? Why not offer to reduce stress and increase productivity of hard-working executives and staff of local companies by providing free "stress-reduction" massage therapy? You could conduct a trial comparing stress-reduction and productivity of massaged versus non-massaged staff. Local media would almost certainly be interested. And if results were extraordinary the national media may well pick up your story.

During the Kosovo conflict in 1999, a 12-year old schoolgirl arranged a concert to raise money for war victims. She sent out a press release and waited in anticipation. Within *days* her press release attracted publicist Max Clifford who committed to help organise the event. Max in turn attracted superstar Michael Jackson to play at her concert, at a major venue. Days later her story was broadcast on the national evening news across the UK.

Has this schoolgirl got a talent most people haven't? NO! She's just an ordinary schoolgirl who had a good idea. The difference between her and hundreds of other school children who might think to put on a charity concert is that *she took action and pursued publicity.*

Most business owners can learn much from her action.

Here are some more unusual angles: if you owned a music store you could *donate all your profit* on sales of the current number one album (and quote the amount you will donate – £4.00 on a CD retailing for £14.00, for instance) and give it to a high profile cause. Do you think this would attract media attention? I bet it would. The free publicity would attract a stream of CD buyers who would likely buy *other* CD's while they are in your store, and return to buy repeatedly in future.

If you were a landscape gardener you could pick a 'theme' like a Roman or Victorian garden, become expert in that period, and gain publicity on your speciality, backed with some interesting, fascinating, or humorous stories of period life in the garden.

If you were an investment broker you could focus on investments particularly suited to people aged 65 and over. Or 30-something couples. Or teenagers.

Imagine — if you could show teenagers how to start investing now, and accrue a net worth of one million pounds by the time they were 45, you'd get publicity!

(As a side note, almost **anyone** can accrue a net million pound fortune within a 20-25 year period by investing just a small daily amount in the right unit trusts, with low risk. Why don't more investment managers publicise this fact?)

Do you see how straightforward it is?

Solve A Problem

This is probably the easiest method of getting free publicity. Solve a problem which, ideally, many people have (although niche market problem solving works, too), and the media will take notice.

Imagine if your product, design or service reduced car crash injury by 50%; solved back, shoulder and neck ache; relieved foot pain; banished obesity; cured depression; resolved insurance inadequacies; stimulated new hair growth; beat crime; halved the cost of heating; restored 20/20 vision; cured phobias — the media would lap it up.

What problem does *your* product or service solve? Describe it in a press release, and tell the world how it works!

Be Eccentric

The media — especially live media — love an unusual personality. Being eccentric can get you a lot of media exposure.

But be careful. Being eccentric does not suit many business identities. So — *as long as it suits your business image* — if you have a particularly strong personality, or you dress strangely, or you have a weird haircut, or you do silly things, include this information in your press release. Media pick up on it because it's different *and will attract more readers, listeners, or viewers* — which is their perpetual goal.

Being eccentric has helped Richard Branson become a master of publicity. And helped Gary Rhodes rocket to the top of his field. It works for them because underlying their eccentricity is great talent. **That is the key.** You use your unusual or extravert personality to attract attention. But then, you must quickly demonstrate your real value or benefit—and that of what you are selling.

Publicity Is More Powerful Than Advertising

To conclude, publicity is **far** more powerful than advertising. And free! Make the pursuit of it a systematic and relentless element of your marketing strategy. It will pay you big dividends.

5-Point Publicity Success Plan

1. Get a high quality list of media sources from your library.
2. Learn to write "killer" press releases, or hire a good direct-response copywriter to do it. Use the "Who cares?" and "What's in it for me?" style of writing.
3. **Fax** press releases to media contacts every week or two.
4. Make outrageous claims you can back up. The media will love it!
5. Get on radio shows with audience call-ins as often as possible.

TIP: When doing radio call-in shows always have something the audience can get from you **free.** Your free giveaway will cement a response and optimize the results of your publicity.

TIP: Never attempt to directly sell anything during your interview. Hosts object to it. Audiences, too, are put off by cheap attempts at salesmanship.

This information is indeed—as promised—worth £10,000-£1,000,000 or more in free advertising. Put a small amount of effort into regularly writing and faxing exciting press releases and watch your sales soar—for free!

BONUS CHAPTER 3

Why You <u>Must</u> Create An Entrepreneurial Business Environment To Achieve — And Maintain — Outstanding Success

About a year ago I decided to buy a second vacuum cleaner with large diameter hoses. We have a large fire and love to keep big logs burning on cold winter days. You can imagine the amount of ash the fire produces. I wanted to be able to pick up ash and bits of bark from the fireplace. A large vacuum would be the answer to easier cleaning.

We had recently received a catalogue from a well known high street catalogue company. It pictured the vacuum we wanted. I phoned to check it was in stock and we set off to reach the store before it closed at 5.30 pm.

We parked outside the store at 5.26 pm — just in time to hurry in and buy our new vacuum.

As we reached the door the staff manager, who was standing by the doors, shut them in our faces!

Worse, as I tried to reason with him through the locked glass doors and explain that it was not even 5.30 pm, *he simply turned his back and walked out of sight!*

He didn't **care.** Not one bit. Zero.

I am usually easy going. But I was *mad* that a national business of this magnitude should allow staff possessing so little interest and motivation even *near* their sales floor. Let alone *manage* it — and blatantly turn away a customer ready to buy.

This level of glaring indifference **doesn't work** in today's sophisticated, customer-driven market place.

As the letter of the law stands, what this store manager did was illegal. When you advertise your opening hours — in ads, in your catalogue, even on your front door — you are required to *be* open for business during the hours you've stated. Not less.

More is fine. Less is *not*.

Technically — if you did what this store manager did — you leave yourself open to legal action. You can be sued for misrepresentation.

But that's not the point. Any business — and I don't care how tiny, medium or large it is — if it wishes to achieve rapid growth, and *continue* to expand and thrive in its field it has to be ruthlessly **customer-oriented.**

As a business owner, you must do everything you humanly can to make it **easy, fast** and **enjoyable** for customers to buy from you. Not shut your doors in their faces at four minutes before closing time.

Joanie's words came back to me when she tried to buy a new modem for her Mac after moving to the UK.

No stockist within an hour's drive, it seemed, had the correct modem. And every UK mail order company's idea of fast delivery was *three days*.

In California, she could have bought a modem from almost any of many Mac dealers, or ordered up until 9.00 pm and received guaranteed next morning delivery from any number of switched-on mail order companies. Attempting to get this fast service in the UK was like trying to introduce primeval man to the concept of flight. It was dire.

Finally, after two solid days of trying to find a modem — which should be readily available from every computer store these days — she slammed the phone down and screamed, "What's the matter with this **** country???"

I am English. I *love* Britain. But Joanie's frustration exposes a serious sluggishness in much of British business. If you've been to America you'll know that, on the whole, businesses are geared up to be efficient, fast and customer-oriented. They *want* your custom. And they *prove* they want it.

US Businesses Reveal Simple Way To Maximise Sales

One simple method by which the majority of businesses in America prove they want your custom is **staying open longer.** They recognise the substantial added sales opportunity of doing so.

Think about it. What hours do the majority of retail and other businesses in the UK operate—including all but a handful of major stores?

Nine until five-thirty, right?

But what hours do the majority of *customers* work?

Nine until five-thirty.

So how on earth do many customers *get into* the shops they want to buy from? They are forced to rush out of work at lunchtime, rush to the shops, rush their purchase, and rush back to work. Or, they shop on the only clear day they can—Saturday.

Is it any wonder lunchtimes and Saturdays in Britain are teaming with hurried shoppers—making the buying experience irritating rather than enjoyable?

As a stark lesson in how **not** to run a business, walk along any high street at around 5.25 pm, Monday to Saturday. What do you notice? Staff standing in doorways, keys in hand, ready to close you out on the dot of 5.30 pm—or sooner, as we found out.

What else do you see at 5.25 pm? *Dozens of hopeful customers trying to get into shops before they close.*

When you walk along most high streets or shopping malls in America at 5.25 pm—you see a very different picture. These stores are not even *thinking* of closing yet. Instead, they're thinking of how much money they can earn from customers pouring out of work at 5.30 pm.

So they stay open until 8.00 or 9.00 pm. Even at nine, if you look as if you're heading their way many will eagerly serve you!

Major supermarkets don't close, period. They are now 24-hour, 7-days-a-week businesses.

Why? Because they recognise that **customers** are the key to their success. You want to shop when **you** want to, not when shops dictate you must. And you want impressive service from those shops. *This is the key to success in the 2000's.*

Train Your Staff To Be Entrepreneurial And Give Them An *Incentive* To Work Hard

Do you suppose the *owner* of the catalogue store would have turned us away? I seriously doubt it. But hasn't he done so just the same by not training and creating incentive for his staff?

The only way he — and any business owner — will ever transform staff from nine-to-five, unmotivated, unreliable 'workers', is to make them **part of the deal.**

You create self-motivated, caring, customer-focused staff by giving them a good **personal and financial** *reason* to be and do their best. To *want* to ethically sell as much product or service as they can everyday, and give higher-level, more enthused service to every customer, client or prospect.

How do you motivate your staff — I'm talking about **all** your staff, not just your sales people — sufficiently to *want* to work longer, *want* to be genuinely friendly, *want* to take the time and effort to help customers make wise buying decisions, *want* to ensure every customer walks away from the transaction having received a highly efficient, enjoyable and memorable experience?

Here are six keys to build a motivated and hard-working team of employees.

KEY #1: Train your staff to think like **entrepreneurs.**

Every soul in your business — from you the owner, right along to your packing, delivery and cleaning staff — must recognise that your **customers or clients** rule each day. I like the Japanese thinking: "In the West, they say the customer is king. In Japan, we say the customer is **god.**"

It's easy for staff to get caught up in what *they do*. The details of *their job*. The larger you grow the more easily you can become inward-focused. Why? Because, the internal activity which makes it possible to supply your customers or clients with whatever it is you sell becomes an organisation in itself. Your staff arrive at your office to do their administration job, or their technical job, or their accounting job, or their database entry job — or their designing, cleaning, researching, maintaining, developing, packing, stock controlling job — or whatever.

They become blinkered — focused only on *their job*.

But 'jobs' are mostly boring. 'Jobs' are uninteresting, tedious, monotonous, and unfulfilling. So staff want to get done as quickly as possible — and only sufficiently well to guarantee their pay cheque at the end of the month, and to leave on the dot of 5.30 pm everyday to get a life.

Can you honestly blame them?

You change staff attitude almost overnight when you create an **entrepreneurial environment** in which each employee understands the value of the role they play in making your business work — and providing your customers or clients with an astonishing service.

How do you achieve it? Explain and demonstrate how everything your employee does affects the result your customer or clients receives — even if what he or she does is part of a *chain* of functions which *eventually* produce a result for your customer.

Let your employee know he or she is important! That they play a vital role in astonishing your customer!

KEY #2: Give each staff member **responsibility.**

People thrive on responsibility. Promote an environment that invites creativity and improvement. You'll be amazed at the number of creative suggestions put forward by staff on how to improve the way you do business — if you encourage it and support the free-flow of ideas.

You don't have to adopt every idea. But you do have to **respect** every idea that's given to you. By doing so you breed trust and confidence in your employees and they'll keep their ideas coming.

When you do take up an idea, congratulate and reward the staff member who gave it you **publicly.** Give him or her a bottle of wine and a 'thank you' card. Or put his or her name on an *Idea of The Month* board for everyone to see. Or give him or her two tickets to see a movie. Or anything else that recognises and appreciates their input.

KEY #3: Give staff the **authority** — and **autonomy** — to make decisions *at their point of work* — within a prescribed domain.

A few days ago I wanted to buy a book. The only copy on the shelf was slightly damaged. I asked the assistant whether she had another. She didn't. But without hesitation, she offered me 20% off the price. I accepted because I didn't want to wait for a copy. I walked away *appreciating the transaction*. That business had taken the time to train staff to be ready for such occurrences, and give them autonomy to make their own decisions, within predetermined parameters.

Authority and autonomy improves staff ability and working satisfaction — and therefore enhances your customer's buying experience, too.

KEY #4: Give continual **feedback.**

Many companies I visit rarely let their employees see the end results of their work. It's like me inviting you to a World Cup tournament and then asking you to leave 30-minutes before the end. The final score completes the tournament — and crowns the experience for you.

Your staff respond to seeing the final score too.

What is the *result* of their staying two hours longer to organise and categorize the new stock? How much added revenue has four busy days at the trade show generated? By what percent have sales increased by keeping your doors open an extra two hours every day? How has the newly designed price list helped customers buy? Your staff want to know!

People gain more satisfaction, become more dedicated, more motivated, and more reliable when they see the fruits of their labour.

KEY #5: Make work **fun!**

Show your staff you *like* and *enjoy* their company. Be a friend to them. Recognise their birthdays, anniversaries, special occasions; their *children's* birthdays and special occasions. Give them Christmas gifts. Take them on trips, meals, special outings.

The old school of management thinking warned you to keep a 'professional' distance from your staff. I warn you **not** to distance yourself from your staff. Here's why. Would *you* do your best work in a sterile and impersonal environment?

Or would you work more productively in a friendly, supportive, *enjoyable* environment?

One of my clients has grown his business from £300,000 to over two million pounds in twelve months. He now employs twenty-three staff. Virtually every employ stays with him long term. Staff attrition is practically zero. And he's in an industry — computers — which traditionally suffers high staff turnover. How does he do it? He makes coming to work fun! He *includes* his staff in the goings-on of his business.

Every Christmas he arranges a fun meal at a commended restaurant. Every Halloween he arranges a fancy dress party. Every Easter he arranges an Easter egg hunt with worthwhile prizes. Every summer he takes his staff on an outing. This year they went punting in Oxford, with prizes for the punter who fell in least! When it's someone's birthday he gifts a nice bottle of wine. When the company wins a new contract he makes sure he celebrates with all his staff.

Do you think it's coincidence that almost no staff leave? They enjoy going to work! They work hard because they are individually recognised and rewarded for their effort.

Make work fun for your employees!

KEY #6: Give your staff **ownership.**

There is no better way of motivating a person than by giving them ownership of what they do — and then reward them financially in direct proportion to the results they achieve.

To give ownership, you must create lots of micro 'businesses' within your macro business — each one being 'owned' and run by each individual or each small team, who is responsible for the results it produces. You decentralise your operation and hand responsibility to individuals.

Here are five ways to give ownership:

1. Give your sales staff a direct cut of the gross sales they generate. The more they sell, the more they earn.

Many companies pay commissions on sales. But not many structure it in the most effective way.

What's the key? To give *generously*.

A salesperson from *Auto Trader* magazine told me a few years ago that John Madejski, the entrepreneur who started the magazine with two thousand pounds, pays all his sales people a basic wage of £4,000. Yet this salesperson was earning in excess of £50,000 a year, £46,000 in commissions. He was keen to stop talking and go and sell more advertising! Do you think John Madejski would be getting the same drive from his sales team if he paid them £25,000 basic plus half the existing commission figures?

Not likely.

2. Give administration, technical, stock control and other 'behind-the-scenes' staff a profit share each quarter, third, or half year — based on a percentage of wages or a cut of your profits.

3. Pay retail staff a percentage of the sales revenue they help to generate. Pay it monthly or quarterly, not less.

4. Pay design and other creative staff a percentage of the fee paid by your client. Pay it when the client pays, or with the following end of month pay cheques.

5. Offer all employees stock options with the ability to cash them in at any time.

Creating an entrepreneurial environment is critical to your success. It enlivens your service with driven employees. It recognizes your customer as being your biggest asset by creating an environment in which each employee has the training and authority to give every customer astonishing service.

The success of Nordstrom is still the best evidence that customer service makes money. Nordstrom run their stores decentralized. Bruce Nordstrom said, "We open a few stores that do $100 million a year in their first year. That's never been done by anybody."

That's the power of entrepreneurial leadership.

WHAT NOW?

What determines whether your business will now grow by the fast pace you want it to?

ACTION!

Every year I have the opportunity to teach thousands of business owners, directors and professionals the powerful marketing techniques you have just discovered — through this book, my monthly *Business Success* newsletter, live seminars, various one-to-one very intense marketing programmes I conduct, and private consultancy.

In almost every case, the businesses which achieve incredible growth — in short time — do so because they are **action-oriented.** They systematically and relentlessly *apply* the powerful marketing strategies that make quantum growth predictable.

My greatest wish is that you will now take what I've taught you and apply it. You **can** build the business or practice of your dreams! Go now and build wealth and a lasting fortune. Live the life of personal and financial riches that is yours for the taking!

One thing. Realise nothing can stop you — other than *yourself.* Smash any misconceptions you have about your worthiness or ability to massively succeed. You can achieve any business result you put your mind to — when — and as soon as — you adopt and apply what I've shown you in these pages.

This quote from Henry Thoreau helps *me* constantly believe anything imagined is achievable :

> If one advances confidently in the direction of his dreams, and endeavours to *live* the life he has imagined, he will meet with a success unexpected in common hours... new, universal, and more liberal laws will begin to establish themselves around and within him... *and he will live with the licence of a higher order of beings.*
>
> If you have built castles in the air, your work need not be lost; that is where they should be. *Now put the foundations under them.*

The foundations of your success are contained in these pages. Simply **apply them now** and get ready to receive abundant results.

Paul Gorman